PARADOXES OF KNOWLEDGE

PARADOXES OF KNOWLEDGE

Elizabeth Hankins Wolgast

Cornell University Press | ITHACA AND LONDON

First published 1977 by Cornell University Press.
Published in the United Kingdom by Cornell University Press Ltd., 2-4 Brook Street, London W1Y 1AA.

International Standard Book Number 0-8014-1090-8
Library of Congress Catalog Card Number 77-3130
Printed in the United States of America by York Composition Co., Inc.
Librarians: Library of Congress cataloging information appears on the last page of this book.

To

Richard
Stephen
Johanna

Acknowledgments

While this work has been in progress my debt to friends, students, and colleagues has grown. I mention here only those whose help was greatest and most recent.

My debt to Norman Malcolm is first in importance: he has read and criticized several parts of this work and helped me to wrestle with various points of error and obscurity. I owe much to the criticisms and encouragement of A. I. Melden, John Goheen, and Wallace Matson. Fred O'Toole's comments on belief-expression were invaluable, as were suggestions by Rush Rhees and Alan White. I profited from the comments made by Alice Ambrose on Chapter VI, and from the help of Willis Doney and Harry Frankfurt with Chapter V. I thank my colleagues at California State University, Hayward, and my Dartmouth seminar students (Bernard Lambek in particular) for their skepticism and suggestions.

I am exceedingly grateful to Georgia Bassen, who edited the manuscript for me. Her philosophical acumen, perspicacity, and tact guided me through many boggy places in the argument. I also thank Newton Garver, who first read the manuscript for Cornell University Press and provided valuable guidance for a final rewriting. Elsie Myers Stainton edited the manuscript for Cornell University Press and is responsible for making countless improvements in the text.

The American Council of Learned Societies awarded me a fellowship for 1970/71, when the project took on its present dimensions and form.

Thanks are due the editor of *The Philosophical Review* for permission to use my paper "Knowing and What It Implies" (vol. 81, July 1971, pp. 360–370), which appears in a revised form as Chapter I, and to George Allen & Unwin for permission to use materials from G. E. Moore's *Some Main Problems of Philosophy*, his *Commonplace Book*, and his *Lectures in Philosophy*.

E. H. W.

Berkeley, California

Analytical Table of Contents

case. Yet the distinction of that case does not allow asking his original question. (3) Malcolm's and Hintikka's interpretations of Prichard are criticized. Underlying these interpretations and Prichard's question is the assumption that knowing has a certain kind of object, and that saying one knows a thing refers to one's relation to that object. However, this assumption does not allow for the shifts of meaning in saying one knows. (4) There is no general distinction between knowing and believing. We may deny that we know in one situation what we claim to know in another, without inconsistency or change in attitude.

(1) Moore frequently gave examples of things he knew, but his use of 'know' in giving them was odd. Does this mean we cannot give natural examples of what we know? (2) Various uses of 'I know' are studied; the force changes with changes in context. None of its uses is appropriate for giving examples. (3) The catalog hypothesis: is there a list of all the things we know? It is a mistake to treat knowledge as a class concept. (4) Many philosophers have supposed there is such a class as 'all the things one knows,' and thought it was one task of philosophy to describe it: Plato, Descartes, Locke, Moore. This assumption is connected with the assumption that knowledge has a certain sort of object. It also derives from taking phrases in ordinary use as describing how a concept works. The procedure of looking at what we say we know as a means of studying the concept of knowledge is defended.

'Moore's paradox': we cannot assert a particular proposition although it is meaningful and may be true. Moore's solution: we imply that we believe what we say. (1) The paradox involves a certain view of meaning; Moore was interested in related questions and paradoxes. (2) The 'package view' of meaning underlies the paradox. The conception of belief-expression and the use of sentences to tell something to someone is presented. (3) What is the connection between truth and belief-expression? Sentences that normally express beliefs are contrasted with mathematical ones. (4) Moore's paradox is evaluated: does it involve a contradiction? It has a crucial feature in common with contradictions. (5) The argument is summarized and its implications considered.

(1) Descartes's purpose was to prove his existence as a first move in establishing knowledge. Various forms of his argument are compared. What is meant by an 'argument for one's existence'? (2) The 'inference' from thinking to existence: a formal argument is distinguished from a proof against doubt. (3) We think we must have a belief in our existence, and therefore a proof of it. Is there such a belief? One argument for thinking there is involves the assumption that, if one proposition entails another, the belief that the former is true entails a belief that the latter is. This assumption is shown to be wrong. (4) The argument of this chapter is summarized. The Appendix offers an explanation of Descartes's curious inconsistencies regarding his proof.

Moore defends Common Sense by asserting that certain propositions are true and known by him. (1) Some of these entail that time is real. The status of Moore's truisms and of 'Time is real' is considered. (2) These propositions are seen not to be expressive of beliefs; therefore their truth or falsity should not concern us. (3) McTaggart's and Bradley's arguments against the reality of time are presented. Their views, like Moore's, are justified by ordinary things we say. What then should be made of their conflict? What is the significance of 'contradiction' in philosophical dispute? (4) Moore's 'defense' of Common Sense is evaluated. Is there a 'Common Sense view'? The nature of inferences leading to propositions like 'Time is real' is discussed.

The first question for the theory of knowledge is sometimes thought to be: What (if anything) is certain? This question leads to skepticism. (1) Why is absolute certainty required? How is such certainty determined? Malcolm's 'strong' and 'weak' senses of 'know' are considered. (2) Saying one knows in the strong sense of 'know' does not close debate; neither do expressions of 'absolute certainty.' Such assertions acknowledge, rather, that debate and challenge are reasonable. We see why Moore's most obvious assertions aroused expressions of doubt. (3) There is no defense against the possibility of doubting what is known, but neither is any defense needed. (4) Defining knowledge implies that what is known, like what is a zebra, is a matter on which there should be agreement among speakers of the language. Our argument shows this is wrong. What is said to be 'known' is always open to challenge. That belongs to the concept of 'knowing.'

PARADOXES OF KNOWLEDGE

You must bear in mind that the language-game is so to say something unpredictable. I mean: it is not based on grounds. It is not reasonable (or unreasonable).

It is there—like our life.

—Wittgenstein, *On Certainty*

Introduction

This work does not present a theory of knowledge, nor does it attempt to define knowledge. It does not consider whether we really know the things we think we do. It neither defends nor attacks the claim that there *is* such a thing as knowledge, nor does it evaluate methods for attaining certainty. Although these things are commonly taken to be concerns of the philosophy of knowledge, I will argue that taking them so is mistaken.

What is offered here is a selection of paradoxes connected with knowledge and belief. For example, a question that apparently ought to have an answer has none; an example that apparently should exist cannot be found; an absurdity stems from a seemingly innocuous sentence; two conflicting arguments are moved by the same kind of inference; absolute certainty seems at once both common and unattainable. In such puzzling matters philosophy fascinates beginning students no less than experienced philosophers. The issues that trouble us most lie near the beginning, close to the surface where we start.

The various issues and their treatment in this work have considerable independence from one another. They apparently cluster around the concepts of knowledge and belief. But one can think of them as segments of a circular figure, so related that we may begin anywhere on the circumference and, exploring inward, come to a common center. For we find assumptions common to and connecting the different issues, and a picture begins to emerge of how these assumptions provide the mechanism for the paradoxes.

The design, or structure, is therefore *post hoc*. It appears with the disclosure of very rudimentary assumptions and their influence on how we view knowledge. Each assumption appears in more than one connection, and so together they form themes running through the whole. This fact is the only justification for saying that there is a 'theory' here. It would be more just perhaps to speak of the book as a mere prolegomenon to a theory of knowledge.

The assumptions themselves are so fundamental that they seem at once obvious and indiscernable. That is to say, they are so obvious as not to be thought of as assumptions; and when brought into focus they strike us as self-evident. Among such assumptions are the following: that there is a class of objects which are the objects of knowledge and belief; that the connections which hold between propositions will normally be reflected in connections holding between the propositions that we *know* those things the propositions assert; that our knowledge has a structure, with foundations supporting the rest; that logical consistency will characterize a true philosophical account; that a paramount concern of epistemology is to judge whether we ever attain certainty. When we have brought these assumptions into critical view, it will be clear that without them the paradoxes dissolve. We have then a powerful motive for mistrusting them. Without them, however, much of what constitutes the philosophy of knowledge would never have been written.

My method is analytic in a Cartesian sense; it proceeds by raising questions and locating the general issues that must enter their answers. The method is not directed toward giving general answers, however, but rather toward seeing how the questions work and how they generate paradoxes. One of the lessons to be learned in this inquiry is that generalizations (for example, about knowledge) bind us in uncomfortable ways. Our desire for generality, as Wittgenstein remarked, leads us into difficulties. When we find an unqualified generalization in philosophy, chances are it will not hold. But then, doesn't it follow that a theory of knowledge cannot be given? If a 'theory' is to describe a structure with principles and proofs, then perhaps such a thing is impossible. But if 'theory' means a description of how concepts work and are related, then no such consequence ensues. We can envision obtaining a clear and true account of how 'know,' 'believe,' 'doubt,' and 'verification' work together, and how these are related to still other concepts. We can imagine a sort of conceptual map. But it would be a mistake to suppose only one map exists relating these. It is more realistic to think of different maps which coexist, transparently as it were, with none obscuring the others. Such a complicated description is possible.

How were the subjects chosen? Not all of them are universally viewed as central to the philosophy of knowledge. Some indeed are thought to be mere curiosities, not important enough to determine the shape of a theory. Others, like the proof that I exist, are considered fundamental. I chose this set because of a feature they all share: each, while severely puzzling, can be presented in the most ordinary terms. Each lies close to ordinary remarks involving 'know' and 'believe,' and can therefore be presented to a beginner in philosophy or a nonphilosopher. Their force is their own, not depending upon acquaintance with a philosophical tradition or mastery of a vocabulary. So it is my hope that this work may be read by that 'common reader' who so influenced the style of English philosophy from Bacon through Berkeley and Hume and Russell, and whose French counterpart Descartes once addressed. Perhaps someone unfamiliar with philosophy will find here something interesting for himself.

A second reason for choosing these issues is related to the first. Issues accessible to common speech and common sense have underpinnings more easily seen and described. They have a simplicity and translucency lacking when philosophy becomes technical. If there is a design relating the concepts of knowledge and belief, one can more surely see it in this context, in connection with these issues.

There is a third consideration, but of less influence than the others. Some of these issues arise repeatedly in the history of philosophy, and historically the philosophy of knowledge might be defined by its perennial concerns. For instance, Prichard raises a question considered by Descartes and even earlier by Plato: What is the difference between knowing and merely believing? Moore, like Plato and Zeno, brought attention to the question: What is the role of contradiction in philosophical reasoning? And Bradley and Moore, as well as Kant and Locke and Parmenides, inquired about our most fundamental assertions, those at the outermost limit of reason's grasp. A work proposing to serve that historical tradition benefits by respecting these ancient and continually puzzling themes.

I have given particular importance to the paradoxical nature of the present disputes. The best account of the role of paradox or contradiction in philosophy is given by Plato in the *Republic:* Contradictions or apparent contradictions force the mind to reflect in unaccustomed ways. Reason is compelled in the face of a contradiction to strive toward a higher level of understanding.[1] Seen this way, paradoxes and contradictions are doors for philosophical discovery—philosophical beginnings, forcing us to reconsider what is self-evident and think of possibilities we would not otherwise conceive of. By

1. Steph. 523–525, in *The Dialogues of Plato,* B. Jowett, trans. (New York: Random House, 1937), I, pp. 782–784.

stumbling on a paradox one may discover that the most innocuous-looking truism is false.

A comment is in order about the influence mathematics and logic have had on the assumptions I deal with, particularly assumptions about propositions and their importance for an account of knowledge. C. I. Lewis, having just worked through *Principia Mathematica*, said of his *Mind and the World Order* that its conceptions grew out of investigations in logic and mathematics:

The historic connection which exists between mathematics and exact sciences on the one hand and conceptions of knowledge on the other, needs no emphasis: from Plato to the present day, all the major epistemological theories have been dominated by, or formulated in the light of, accompanying conceptions of mathematics. Nor is the reason for this connection far to seek; mathematics, of all human affairs, most clearly exhibits certitude and precision.[2]

The strong historical connection that does exist, as Lewis says, between epistemology and discoveries in mathematics can be found in the works of many thinkers from Zeno and Plato onward. However, this 'connection' often assumes a great deal about the nature of knowledge, and the assumptions deriving from mathematics are as often as not pernicious. For through them mathematics easily comes to stand as the model of all knowledge; other kinds of knowledge are made to fit it, or failing to, lose their claim to count as knowledge. The admiration philosophers have felt toward mathematical proofs and formal systems has often clouded their vision of other and more immediate ways of talking about what we know. It has proved a heavy handicap, I argue.

Of the philosophers considered here, G. E. Moore, is more frequently referred to than any other. Moore was fascinated

2. *Mind and the World Order* (New York: Dover, 1956), p. vii.

with paradoxes of various kinds—the liar, the Epimenides, and other paradoxes of his own description. In his notes he turns repeatedly to them, trying to get at their source. His interest in paradoxes was not so much in getting rid of them, like nuisances in the way of a general thesis, as in seeing what truth they obscured. He exemplifies the philosopher who takes paradoxes as doors to the truth. Moore also was interested in the relation of philosophy to common sense—to a philosophically untutored perspective. When forced to take sides, he generally chose what he thought represented common sense even when he could not resolve the philosophical difficulties attendant on that choice. Paradoxes connected with such common-sense positions bothered him greatly. He respected them. And he respected their origins in common sense more than he did the most tyrannical logical 'necessities.' Further, unlike Lewis, who took philosophical ideas from mathematics and logic, Moore's discussions always began from the informal and common sense side of the boundary between "certain and precise" systems and the unsystematic, pragmatic language of everyday use. In this approach Moore can, I think, be shown to be right, and I have tried to show that.

Something must be said about my terminology with respect to the words 'sentence,' 'proposition,' 'statement,' and 'assertion.' It has become normal philosophical practice to distinguish 'sentences' and 'propositions' in such a way that sentences may be uttered, but only propositions asserted; sentences may be meaningful, but only propositions may be true; sentences may express something, but what they express is propositions; sentences but not propositions may be ambiguous. To distinguish so sharply between a sentence and the proposition it 'expresses' runs directly against a claim I want to make and support: that for many sentences, one aspect—the most important aspect—of their meaning lies in the patterns of their use, and these patterns can only very misleadingly be called 'propositions.' So even though one aspect of meaning has to do with the logical connections between a form of words and other related forms, this connection is more plausibly thought of as holding between *sentences*. Maintaining the distinction between sentences and propositions, which dictates that only propositions have meaning, would prohibit our distinguishing these two dimensions of meaning. It would not allow speaking of 'the meaning' of a form of words on the one hand, nor would it allow us to investigate a pattern of use as an investigation of meaning on the other. Yet both of these are essential parts of the description of the concepts 'know' and 'believe.' Furthermore, the sentence-proposition distinction easily leads to the claim that a proposition is a common object of belief, a claim I am anxious to deny.

The solution to this terminological difficulty cannot be found in a consistent use of 'statement' or 'assertion' in place of 'sentence' or 'proposition.' For several of the paradoxes concern sentences (or propositions) which are never uttered— at least not outside philosophy. Therefore to call them 'statements' or 'assertions' and so treat them as having an ordinary use and function seems plainly wrong. My practice has been to use whichever term seems most natural in a given context, for example, to limit 'statement' and 'assertion' to something really stated or asserted. Sometimes I refer to 'There is a watch on the table' as a sentence, sometimes as a proposition; my choice often depends upon what I am saying *about* 'There is a watch on the table,' since philosophical usage would forbid saying certain things of that sentence and would forbid saying other things about that proposition. My justification for so mixing up terms is that I believe one *can* say of 'There is a watch on the table': that it is uttered or asserted; that it is meaningful and perhaps true; that it might be ambiguous; that it entails other things like it, whatever they are to be called; and that it normally expresses belief. To say that it 'expresses a proposition' does not seem either so clear or so natural as any of these. In order to cut through what I believe is a wrong distinction, I have had to avoid observing it. To have practiced observing it would have been a commitment to its propriety.

Although it doesn't present a thesis, this work has a positive aspect, for it reveals links that connect concepts, links that are visible only from a certain angle and under a certain light. Once seen, they help change our ideas of how the concepts must work, and our attitudes about the concepts then begin to change. If, for instance, one sees that the notion of a 'class of things we know' participates in several paradoxical lines of argument, that notion begins to seem less self-evident. It seems less indispensable. Could we do without it? What would be the consequences? These questions press for answers. My argument at this point resembles one that is characteristic of G. E. Moore: if an assumption leads to paradoxes close to home, in our ordinary speech and the everyday expression of our beliefs, this is a powerful reason to let it go—(not for denying it, as Moore sometimes does; that may lead to paradox too). When one sees how much order naturally results from relaxing one's hold on such an assumption, the possibility of getting along without it becomes attractive. It is not so difficult after all. We simply lose our compulsion to reason in the old way.

I

Knowing and What It Implies

A common type of argument is given to show that we do not know all that we think we do: For instance, if I say that I know there is a watch on the table, then, although I see one there, I would be asserting more than I really know. For what I say implies that something on the table has a watchworks inside, and I certainly mean to imply this. Yet I have not looked inside the watch; and if someone asked me whether I *know* that a certain object there has a watchworks in it I would say I do not. Therefore, since having such a works is a necessary condition for that object being a watch, it follows that I did not know there was a watch on the table as I said.

The general form of argument of which this is an instance is ubiquitous in writings on the nature of knowledge. The form can be described this way: we claim to know things whose consequences we deny knowing; yet this denial indicates our uncertainty, and from this it follows that we do not know what we claim. It has often appeared as an argument about perceptual knowledge, as it does in Descartes's discussion of how he knows he has before him a piece of wax. At first he proposes that he knows it because he sees it.

> I chanced, however, to look out of the window, and see men walking in the street; now I say in ordinary language that I 'see' them, just as I 'see' the wax; but what can I 'see' besides hats and coats which may cover automata?[1]

What he sees, and what we would see, are only moving hats and coats and shoes, with perhaps the merest glimpse of what we take to be a face. Aren't we jumping to conclusions if we infer that we see people? We are ignorant of what goes on beneath the surface or on the far sides of things. Although we can turn things over and look inside, the fact is we don't do this ordinarily before asserting that we know what they are. In making such assertions, then, we assert more than we really know.

A more recent version of the argument is given by C. D. Broad:

> It would be admitted by every one that a bell is something more than a coloured surface, more than a cold hard surface, and so on. Now, so long as I merely look at a bell, its colour only is revealed to me; its temperature or hardness are certainly not revealed in the same sense at that time. . . . I have no right to say that the *bell* is a constituent of [my] perceptual situation. At most I may say there is a constituent which displays certain qualities, and that this same constituent has in fact other qualities which would be displayed under other conditions.[2]

Seeing a bell is seeing an object with many qualities besides visual ones. How do we know by looking that there is a bell before us? Strictly speaking we do not. Saying we see a bell implies more than we know to be the case. It implies that

1. G. E. M. Anscombe and P. Geach, trans. and eds., *Descartes: Philosophical Writings* (Edinburgh: Nelson and Sons, 1954), p. 73.

2. *Mind and Its Place in Nature* (New York: Humanities Press, 1951), pp. 149–150.

other nonvisual qualities would be perceived under other circumstances. It is only one step from this to the verificationist form of the argument—the form according to which saying one sees a bell is saying something by implication about a great number of things occurring in the future. Yet obviously these future events are not known to us now. Therefore we do not, strictly speaking, know what we assert.

The argument can take many forms unrelated to perception. For example, a man who says he knows where his car is parked is asked if he knows it has not been towed away in the past ten minutes. To this he answers that he does not. Then, he is told, he should not have said he knew where it was. Or consider this example: Someone asserts that all squirrels eat nuts. He is asked if he knows this of every squirrel which ever lived. Bewildered he confesses he does not. Aha, he is told, then you should not have said you knew.

I believe this form is at work in Hume's famous argument about induction:

The bread, which I formerly eat, nourished me; that is, a body of such sensible qualities was, at that time, endued with such secret powers: but does it follow, that other bread must also nourish me at another time, and that like sensible qualities must always be attended with like secret powers? The consequence seems nowise necessary. At least, it must be acknowledged that there is here a consequence drawn by the mind; that there is a certain step taken; a process of thought, and an inference, which wants to be explained.[3]

If I believe or assert that this bread is nourishing, it is because I think all bread (resembling bread I have eaten in the past) will nourish me. But I cannot know this. Therefore I cannot know that this bread is nourishing. The best we have is probability, and this Hume explains as a kind of habit.

3. *Enquiries Concerning the Human Understanding*, L. A. Selby-Bigge, ed. (Oxford: Oxford University Press, 1951), p. 34.

Being determined by custom to transfer the past to the future, in all our inferences; where the past has been entirely regular and uniform, we expect the event with the greatest assurance, and leave no room for any contrary supposition. But where different effects have been found to follow from causes, which are to *appearance* exactly similar, all these various effects must occur to the mind in transferring the past to the future, and enter into our consideration, when we determine the probability of the event.[4]

We judge the bread as we do the watch by its appearance and by our experience with like-appearing things. But we do not know anything more about it than its appearance. We do not know what we commonly think we do.

The argument is curious when compared to our practice. We find it quite natural to say we 'know' a thing such as where our car is parked; and the question, "But do you know it hasn't been towed away?" brings forward no evidence that it has been towed. It does not make one think: "Oh yes, perhaps it was towed away, being parked by the red curb." The question has not changed anything or reminded us of anything we overlooked. Rather it seems to be directed against our use of 'know' or our confident manner of assertion. That use or that manner is made to seem careless, incautious. We seem to be chided about it.

Yet despite the argument, philosophers, like everyone else, go right on using 'know' in the way under fire.[5] Even more significant and curious is that it would be absurd to do otherwise. It would be absurd to refrain from saying one knows there is a watch unless one has taken it apart. And it would be at least neurotic to run and look before asserting positively where one's car is parked. If this is so, then why should any-

4. *Ibid.*, p. 58.
5. That philosophers should, in their everyday speech, belie a conclusion they endorse is a phenomenon Moore found particularly puzzling. It will be discussed in another connection in Chapter VI.

one feel embarrassment about using 'know' in the usual way? Why does anyone feel he is being inconsistent in this use? The source of this is hidden, and we seem to have no defense against its effect.

1

Let us see exactly how the argument works. Let
  A = There is a watch on the table.
  B = There is an object containing watchworks on the table.

In conformity with common philosophical usage, we can say that A implies (or entails) B. A implies other things as well: for example, it implies that the works are connected with something on the face and produce whatever happens on the face. Now in saying the one thing implies the other we mean that if the latter is false that will make the former false. If B is false, A will be false. I do not see any difficulty here. A further remark is often made of such an implication as this. It is said that B is a necessary condition for A, that there being a watchworks inside is a necessary condition for something being a watch. This claim will have to be carefully considered.

Now let us consider the relation between these further propositions:
  A_1 = I believe that A.
  B_1 = I believe that B.

It would be generally agreed that A_1 implies (or entails) B_1. Given that A implies B, and that the speaker understands this, it would normally be thought to *follow* that if he believes the one he will believe the other. So that, if he says he believes the one, he shows himself willing to affirm that he believes the other. And so if he were asked whether he believes B subsequent to his assertion that he believes A, he would answer that of course he does. It would often be said too, though not as unequivocally as before, that believing B is a necessary condition for believing A. It is a necessary condition at least for any speaker who understands that A does imply B.

Now consider still a third pair of propositions:

A_2 = I know that A.
B_2 = I know that B.

How are these related? Does A_2 imply or entail B_2? Does saying or asserting A_2 entail that one is willing to assert B_2? If it does, then it would be inconsistent to assert the former and deny the latter. Can B_2 be thought of as the assertion of a necessary condition to the truth of A_2? If so, then again it would be inconsistent to assert the latter and deny the former. These questions go to the crux of the argument before us.

We notice, of course, that A_2 unequivocally implies A, and by the transitivity of implication, also implies B. And this is indeed reflected in the way we speak. Someone who asserts that he knows there is a watch on the table would surely not deny there is a watch there; nor would he deny that something on the table contains a watchworks. He would say "Of course!" to questions about either of these things. But this does not tell us how to answer the main question whether *asserting* A_2 commits us to asserting B_2 on being asked.

When one sentence implies another it is sometimes said that the second is somehow contained in the first, or is included in or is part of the first. The sentence A is thought of as saying more than B, for it implies other things as well as B. And B does not say all that A does, nor imply A. There might be a watchworks inside a music box on the table. B's truth will not guarantee A's.

The idea that knowing B is a necessary condition for knowing A can be explained by analogy to this example. If I know the names of all states in the United States and their capital cities, it follows that (*a*) I know the names of all the states; (*b*) I know the names of all the capitals; and (*c*) I know which capital-name goes with which state-name. Knowing these three things constitutes knowing the states and their capitals. Each of the conditions (*a*), (*b*) and (*c*) is necessary, and together they are sufficient. Nothing is left out or ambiguous. One can think of what is known here as being composed of these parts, and one can think of the knowing as having three parts as well. Each part of the thing known has a corresponding part in the composition of the knowing.

This example illustrates the way we would like to treat all cases of purported knowing, among them knowing that there is a watch on the table. The parts of the proposition *A* will have corresponding members in A_2, among them B_2 inasmuch as *B* constitutes a necessary condition and part of *A*. Let us try to analyze *A* into its parts then. It implies, besides the existence of a watchworks within, that the object possesses a face on which numbers are indicated or appear, and that the changes on the face are related roughly to the time of day.

There are two difficulties with this example, however, which were not present in the other. First, each proposition implied by *A* must refer to the same thing—to a single object. It will not do if one thing on the table has a watchworks in it and another has the face of a watch and still a third changes with the time of day. The propositions implied by *A* are not independent of one another. Therefore it is unclear how they could be thought to constitute *A* by simply being added or taken together. And if they cannot constitute *A* in this way, should they be considered parts of *A* at all? The model of states with capitals fails us here.

Second, it is easy enough to check and see that the names of all the states, the names of all the capitals and the correct pairing of a state with its capital, all add up to exactly what is known when one knows all the states and their capitals. But do we have reason for thinking there is always such a sum? When, for instance, have we got all that is contained in 'There is a watch on the table?' Must the watch face have numerals, or reveal numbers? No—some watches have only marks on their faces. Must there be hands? No—some watches are digital. Must it be running, might it not be broken? One feels bewildered how to answer this. For as there are broken watches, why not a watch whose works are simply missing? That too seems possible. We are rightly baffled. And what our bafflement shows is that the search for a sum or totality here is wrong. It shows that we are wrong in supposing there must be a set of necessary conditions—together being sufficient—for something being a watch. And then it would seem reasonable that there is no set of necessary and sufficient conditions for *knowing* that something is a watch.

Of course we know sometimes that a watch is on the table. But we do not make use of a set of necessary and sufficient conditions to determine it. If, as has been argued, there is no set of conditions from which it follows that someone is in pain, that conclusion should not lend mystery to statements about pain.[6] It is true of other kinds of statements as well, statements with no special claim to mystery. This argument also shows that something is wrong with the verificationist idea that there is a set—albeit perhaps infinite—of future observations entailed by every statement about material things. There often is no set, and so no infinite one.

It is worth distinguishing my argument from an argument that the consequences of *A* are or might be infinite. If we could say all that a watch should look like and do and what sort of works it should have, there would not remain an endless number of other implications to consider. The number of consequences may be rather small. But the conditions themselves are obscure, and their apparent lack of necessity is baffling. This situation will be clearer if we consider a truth about numbers, for instance, that the product of two positive

6. Norman Malcolm makes this point with regard to pain statements and the question whether there are necessary and sufficient conditions for saying someone is in pain. See his "Wittgenstein's *Philosophical Investigations*," included in *Knowledge and Certainty* (Englewood Cliffs, N.J.: Prentice-Hall, 1963), esp. pp. 114–117.

integers will be another positive integer. This proposition implies an infinite number of particular propositions, each of which might be given the form: *n* is a positive integer and *m* is also, and so $n \times m$ will be a positive integer as well. So if one *could* exhaust all these one *should* have all that is contained in the first proposition. Furthermore, we have no hesitation in saying that each of these infinitely many propositions must be true if the general one is, nor do we feel any indecision about what sentences are and what are not implied by the general one. That is to say, we can understand the notion of a sum here even though it is infinite, and we can speak of 'all that is implied' even though we cannot list all that is.

The difference between this example and the watch example is that a proposition like *A*—i.e. a simple factual one— may not follow from any particular set of propositions implied by it. This result provides the key to arguments concerning clever fakes and phony things. An object that looks like a tomato might not be one. Must we cut it to be sure? Or eat it? At what point is it unquestionable that it is a tomato? There is no set of conditions from which it follows that we have a tomato and not a clever imitation. Or a very cleverly made automaton might be dressed to look like a man. At what point, under what circumstances, are we perfectly certain which it is? When he speaks? When he flinches at being struck? No set of conditions is necessary and sufficient. Knowing that something is not a fake does not involve such a set, and this fact makes such knowing seem puzzling and even doubtful. The significance of the argument, however, is to show that some concepts are of this kind: they are not associated with a set of necessary and sufficient conditions.

It is possible that the watch is not really a watch, but a secret microphonic spying device. If we keep to examples that permit clever fakes, the problems associated with their lack of necessary and sufficient conditions will obscure the main skeptical force of the argument. Therefore, I will turn away from such examples to examples that do not have this feature. There are empirical statements which have a definite set of implications, and which can be said to have necessary and sufficient conditions. In the light of such an example we can see more clearly how the argument works.

2

Suppose I frequently see in the park an old woman accompanied by a young child. The child addresses the woman as "Grandmother." The woman is evidently fond of the child. On pointing them out one day I am told by a mutual friend that they are indeed grandmother and grandchild. I remark as I return home that now I know that they are related.

The proposition 'X is grandmother of Y' does not involve an indefinite set of implications. It implies that X is female, that she has (or had) at least one child, and that that offspring is parent to Y. That is all it implies. Each of these conditions is necessary and together they are sufficient. There is obviously no room here for a clever fake.

Now the skeptical question follows this reasoning: You say you know that the woman is grandmother to the child, and if this is so, the woman is someone's mother. Do you know this? Do you have any evidence she is? If not, strange then to imply it. And if she is not anyone's mother, of course she cannot be a grandmother. Therefore you should not have said you *knew* she was.

Notice that these questions do not attack the evidence one has for one's claim, nor do they cast doubt on whether what was asserted is so. The attack seems directed against the use of 'know' to assert something whose consequences one cannot say one knows. The point is to shake the confidence of the speaker in saying he knew.

The effect of the argument is often to make one re-examine the evidence. Was it sufficient? Of course it might have been much stronger. But looking at the evidence will not reveal how the argument works. It works by assuming that one *must say he knows* whatever follows from what he claims to know. No matter how strong the evidence is, we can easily imagine the speaker in our example saying that no, he does not *know* that the woman is a parent. The dissonance between the answers to two questions about knowing remains. If *A* (the woman is grandmother to the child) implies *B* (the woman is someone's parent), then *knowing A* would appear to imply *knowing B*. Yet this the speaker seems to deny when he answers "No."

In an ordinary situation, outside a philosophical discussion, the question whether the speaker knew that the woman is a parent would seem very curious. Did the questioner not hear correctly? Perhaps one should repeat the statement. Perhaps one should ask for an explanation of the question. What does it mean? A philosopher who says he is just asking, having no evidence himself one way or the other and no opinion about it, leaves us extremely puzzled. We would be justified, I think, in giving no answer. Yet we generally feel that there *is* a right answer and that the answer is: we don't know.

What ordinary interpretation of the question lies behind this inclination to say we don't know? If someone asks this question in an ordinary situation, we expect some grounds for doubt to lie behind it. It is the prologue to showing that perhaps we were wrong. 'Do you know there are works in that watch?' might be accompanied by, 'Well, *I* looked and found snuff instead.' So we take the question to be connected to some evidence or proof relevant to its subject. We interpret it, therefore, as a question about *our* awareness of *this* evidence. Inasmuch as it is independent of the evidence we have, our answer is, properly, that we don't know it.

The question 'But do you know that she is a parent?' asks for something independent of our evidence that the woman is a grandmother. That is how we normally take it, and that is why we are inclined to answer that we don't know. But this does not clearly dispose of the argument. For the question remains whether it is consistent for us to answer in this way. If we deny knowing that *B*, which is implied by *A*, must we not confess that we did not know *A* at all? I propose to argue that both remarks are correct and, in this context, quite consistent. I propose that the meaning of these assertions, and in particular the second, derives from the background against which each is made.

Consider changing the example in one respect: Someone asks me if I know whether the woman in the park is a parent or not. I answer to this that I know she is because I know she is a grandmother. Here I have answered the question about *B* by referring to my knowledge that *A*. But if I could do this here, why couldn't I have done the same thing before, against the skeptical question? The answer is that the two questions have different import, and their answers as well. Because the questions are phrased the same we cannot infer that their answers are the same. When I am asked whether I know that *B*, *subsequent* to my asserting that I know that *A*, the question is whether I have independent evidence for *B*. Of course I might have, but it often happens I do not. Therefore, it is quite consistent for me to say I don't know here. It is not inconsistent with saying I know that *A*, for the present question concerns evidence which was not evidence for *A*. Now the relation between knowing *A* and knowing *B* is quite different where I have *not* asserted *A*. There I appear to derive knowing *B* from knowing *A*. The conclusion is inescapable that 'I know' is a phrase whose meaning shifts against different backgrounds; it is context-sensitive.

Reflect on the third-person form—'he knows.' Imagine you assert that Jones knows where his car is parked, meaning that he remembers having parked it and that it is still there. Now, suppose you are asked, "Does Jones know it has not been towed away in the last ten minutes?" This question would strike you as new, concerning evidence independent of what you had for Jones knowing about his car. It raises the question whether the car has been moved and whether Jones might suspect it. This question has to be treated separately from the first one. It needs separate treatment not only when addressed to Jones, but when addressed to you.

This ordinary pattern involving the sentences 'I know that *A*' and 'I know that *B*,' which finds the latter independent of the former, is not reflected in the use given them by philosophers. The philosophical question, as we have seen, does not relate to independent evidence. Rather it requires us to imagine that the two sentences are not separate, but connected. It treats them as if they belonged in a very different situation. It treats them as if the one *should be* derivable from the other, as *B* is derivable from *A* and knowing *B* may be derived from knowing *A* before a question is addressed to whether *B* is known. By juxtaposing a common meaning with a philosophical inquiry we give the appearance of saying something inconsistent. But the truth is that the philosophical use of the question is incongruous with its real use. We are wrong to conclude that a person should retract what he said he knew.

The way to rebut the argument is, therefore, to persist unshaken in what it would be natural and normal to say. For if a speaker loses confidence and now treats what he said he knew with hesitation and doubt, he loses the only play that counts. When he hesitates, it surely follows that he doesn't know.

3

The conclusion which follows is that 'know' and the phrases containing it and questions concerning it, in both the first- and third-person forms, shift with shifting contexts. It would be quite plausible to make the following objection: you either know something or don't know it, and that is what concerns us here—not the way people may or may not use the phrase 'I know.' Obviously someone may use that phrase differently in different situations. But what we are interested in is whether he knows or not.[7] One response to this is: All right, which do you want to say of someone who says he doesn't know *B* after saying he does know *A*?[8] Do you want to say he knows *B of course*, since he knows *A*? Or, in view of his own denial that he knows *B*, would you say he doesn't know it? There is a conflict of criteria here. One criterion leads one way, the other another. That is the important philosophical point.

If we took 'knowing the names of the states and their capitals' as the model for knowing something, then knowing what is implied by knowing this would be part of knowing the whole. It would follow from the fact that one knows the whole that he knows each of the parts. But 'knowing' does not always work this way, even where what is implied is a clear and recognizable set of things. In such cases someone can naturally deny knowing what is implied by what he said he

7. Philosophers are so inclined to make this faulty inference that it is sometimes enunciated as a principle. Hintikka, for example, writes: "Suppose that a man says to you, 'I know that *p* but I don't know whether *q*,' and suppose that *p* can be shown to entail logically *q* by means of some argument which he would be willing to accept. Then you can point out to him that what he says he does not know is already implicitly in what he claims he knows. If your argument is valid, it is irrational for our man to persist in saying that he does not know whether *q* is the case" (J. Hintikka, *Knowledge and Belief* [Ithaca, N.Y.: Cornell University Press, 1962], p. 31). See also David Coder's "Thalberg's Defense of Justified True Belief," *Journal of Philosophy*, 67 (1970), 424–425. There Coder proposes a principle "PDK" making this connection, a principle which Coder calls "unexceptionable" (p. 424). It will be clear on my argument that one cannot make such a general statement about the connection between knowing (being ready to say one knows) a certain thing and knowing (being ready to say one knows) what is implied by it.

8. This assumption enters into other arguments to be discussed subsequently, for example, in Chapter III, Sections 2 and 3.

knew, and he can do this without inconsistency. 'Someone *can* do this' means that the one remark does not preclude the other. Its meaning is not tied to the other. Where we do not have a part-whole relationship in the thing or matter known, we have the normal situation. Therefore, to suppose that questions about knowing and their answers are *always* related in that particular way is the same as supposing that the part-whole relationship *always* characterizes a thing's relation to what it implies. And this assumption is false.

We have most of us felt baffled when a philosopher raised the question whether we *knew* something which is implied by what we had said we knew. It was as if he misunderstood us. Now it is clearer why we have this feeling. For, without introducing his own evidence or proof, he uses a question which normally is connected with these. He is 'just asking.' And we feel the question must have a plain answer. So we answer as we would if the question were used in the normal way and there were evidence behind the question. But now the crucial move has been played. Having caught us in an 'inconsistency,' the skeptic infers that we do not know as we first claimed to. But what is wrong here is not our inconsistency, but his strange use of the question. It is not a question to be 'just asked.' It goes with something before and something after. We are misled by the idea that its meaning is there on its face, and that an answer to it must be unequivocal.

'Know' and phrases containing it take on and discard implications as the contexts in which they occur vary. Their functioning is complicated, and these complications are the materials for other paradoxes which we will consider. We need to be watchful of simplifying assumptions. What Wittgenstein said in connection with 'meaning' applies to 'know' as well:

It is these words which cause most philosophical troubles. Imagine some institution: most of its members have certain regular functions, functions which can easily be described, say, in the statutes of the institution. There are, on the other hand, some members who are employed for odd jobs, which nevertheless may be extremely important. —What causes most trouble in philosophy is that we are tempted to describe the use of important "odd-job" words as though they were words with regular functions.[9]

9. *The Blue and Brown Books* (New York: Harper, 1958), pp. 43–44.

II

Do I Know or Only Believe?

H. A. Prichard wrote about "the fundamental nature of the difference between knowing and believing" that "when we know something we either do, or by reflection can, know that our condition is one of knowing that thing, while when we believe something, we either do or can know that our condition is one of believing and not of knowing, so that we cannot mistake belief for knowledge or vice versa." The difference between them is not one of degree but of kind, he says: "Knowing and believing differ in kind as do desiring and feeling, or as do a red colour and a blue colour."[1]

1

To distinguish knowing from believing is an ancient philosophical enterprise. Plato asked Meno to compare a person who knew the way to Larisa to one who only had a true opinion about it: "And while he has true opinion about that

---

1. *Knowledge and Perception* (London: Oxford University Press, 1950), pp. 88, 87.

which the other knows, he will be just as good a guide if he thinks the truth, as he who knows the truth?" Meno eventually admits to wondering "that knowledge should be preferred to right opinion—or why they should ever differ."[2] There is of course a difference but it does not lie in how useful a guide the one man is as against the other. The difference apparently lies within the possessor. Here in the *Meno*, Plato draws the distinction by asserting that the man who knows has his view secured by reasons, which will prevent him from changing his mind, while the man who has only a true opinion has something which may "play truant and run away". For this reason true opinions are not to be valued, while knowledge, which is secured by "the tie of the cause," is abiding and valuable. Not until the *Theaetetus* does Plato acknowledge that this way of defining knowledge is circular, requiring us to have knowledge (of reasons) as a condition for having knowledge.[3] Nevertheless the nature of his answer indicates that he too thought of the difference between knowing and believing as pertaining to a person's state or condition.

If the difference is internal, can a man discern it for himself? A person says of himself 'I know' or 'I believe' with authority. He must have some way of determining which to say. And what determines him must be part at least of what distinguishes knowing and believing.

If a man determines for himself whether to say 'I know' or 'I believe' in ordinary situations, it is natural a philosopher should look to himself to see how he makes the distinction. This is the procedure followed by Descartes. He asks, what distinguishes those of my ideas which are certain from those which are not? He looks to the ideas themselves for the answer; where else should he look? And the answer he gives us is that the certainly true ideas are those which are perfectly

2. Plato, *Meno*, Steph. 97, I, 377.
3. *Theaetetus*, Steph. 209, II, p. 216.

clear and distinct; these are the ones which are evident to him and certain. The others are not to be trusted on their face.

Prichard follows in this tradition, set by Plato and narrowed by Descartes. We all surely know the difference between knowing and believing. We use it all the time, every time we answer that we believe or that we know something. Then what sort of distinction is it? What can one say about it? Prichard says two things: it is not a difference in degree, and it is to be discovered by reflection or introspection. The first claim is plausible because we do not in fact say that knowing is more or less—for example, 'I am more knowing than believing it.' In our speech the distinction is sharp, just as Prichard says. It is like distinguishing red and blue, not like distinguishing light blue from medium blue. So he calls it a difference in kind. Prichard's second distinction is plausible because, after all, where else does one have to look when one determines whether to say 'I know' or 'I believe'? Someone could rightly answer this with his eyes and ears and other senses stopped. As we discern color differences by looking at the colors, so in a similar way it appears that we can discern the differences in our states by reflecting on them.[4]

This is a tempting line of thinking about knowledge and belief, and its roots lie in ordinary talk of these things. But a difficulty in it is also plain: no matter what a person's state, his belief that something is so might be wrong. Descartes's perfectly clear and distinct ideas might for all he knows be false. Plato's man with the firm and fastened opinion may be

4. We cannot always determine our states by reflection, of course, not our state of insolvency or of matrimony, for two instances. Although Prichard does not make clear what he means by 'state or condition,' he certainly means something which is at least in part subjective. Believing and knowing are in part subjective, as the states mentioned above are not. Hence reflection would naturally pertain to them while not to the others.

simply stubborn. Where someone is mistaken yet very positive of being right, his reflection will not show him his error. How could it? As Norman Malcolm put it: "Where, in these cases, is the material that reflection would strike upon? There is none."[5] In such cases reflection is irrelevant.

In order to be assured that we are distinguishing the right states, those of knowing and believing, we should need assurance that one of them is knowing. We should need to know prior to our reflection that which reflection is supposed to show—that is, whether our state *is* one of knowing. And we have a vicious circle again.

This objection notwithstanding, it seems quite impossible that the distinction between knowledge and belief should be external. For in such a case one's answer whether one knows or believes a thing might involve an investigation *of that thing*. If asked whether I know or believe a certain bush is an azalea, I would not answer with an investigation; the question concerned whether *I knew*. But then what tells me how to answer? Surely I *can* answer it and determine it for myself. But now the question is how do I do it. Do I determine this by introspection or reflection?

2

As the problematic reasoning begins with our observation about the ordinary, everyday use of the phrases 'I know' and 'I believe,' that is where we need to return for its solution. How do we make the distinction between knowing and believing? I don't mean by what marks, or using what method; that there are marks or method has yet to be shown. Rather, how do 'I know' and 'I believe' work in ordinary situations, in situations where either phrase would be as appropriate as the other, where a person has or seems to have a clear choice which to say? If a method or marks exist, if 'reflecting' really

5. "Knowledge and Belief," included in *Knowledge and Certainty*, p. 60.

is involved, we should find the evidence of these things in an ordinary kind of case.

I propose to examine several kinds of situations in which a person might say either 'I know' or 'I believe' in answer to some question. If in these situations we can understand the contrast between knowing and believing, we can see more clearly the nature of the distinction.

Case 1. In a classroom a teacher asks, "What is the capital of Australia?" One student says he knows it's Canberra; another says he believes it's Canberra. Both are right, just as Plato's two guides were right about the way to Larisa. What function is served by the phrases 'I know' and 'I believe'? What, for example, does the teacher make of these two answers? Must he say that the one student knew but the other only believed? He might do this, but he might also say they both knew.

There is enormous confusion for the philosophy of knowledge in the actual use of 'know' and 'believe.' One wants to say: either there is a difference or there is none, but not both. Yet our actual use is such that in the situation described a person might say either that both students knew or that only one did.

What distinction would be made, then, if we *did* distinguish between these students on the basis of how they use 'I know' and 'I believe'? If we said that only one student *knew* the answer, we would mean that only one was *sure* of his answer. The other was hesitant and unsure. For this is the difference conveyed by their answers. If one says 'I know' in this situation, he expresses or communicates confidence; if he says 'I believe,' he communicates lack of it.

How does this contrast fit Prichard's remarks about knowledge and belief? Is it clear that the students' answers pertain to something they reflected on or may have reflected on? That might be the case. A student might pause before answering and ponder, and then say that he knows or that he believes. Would this illustrate the difference between knowing and be-

lieving that Prichard calls attention to? No. For although
there is pondering and perhaps reflection in such a case, the
pondering and reflection seem to concern a difference of degree, not of kind. After pondering, the student might say:
"I'm fairly sure, but not very sure" or "I'm nearly certain,
but not absolutely." And such remarks suggest very strongly
that what he expresses is only the degree of his certainty. This is
even clearer if you imagine him pondering or deliberating at
some length, in an attempt to say exactly how sure he is. If
Prichard had in mind such a case as this, he would never have
said that knowing and believing are as different as red and
blue, or as desiring and feeling. No pondering is relevant to
these! We still need to find a distinction between knowing
and believing which exhibits both features of Prichard's account. Let us look at another case.

Case 2. Imagine a group of people discussing one of the
following topics: whether there is a divine being, whether
there is communication with the dead, whether there is an
ethic of war, whether there are nonearthly rational beings. In
such discussions it is not uncommon for a person to say he
knows that the matter stands one way or the other instead of
saying he believes it does. And yet, even though people speak
this way, we are very much inclined to say that all they express here are their opinions. We are inclined to say that
whether one says one 'strongly believes' or 'knows for certain' here makes no difference. Both are expressions—similar
expressions—of a conviction.[6] But if that were so, why should

6. Should such examples as these count in a discussion of knowledge? Wittgenstein, for one, has suggested that religious beliefs are
utterly unlike "ordinary" ones and that we don't speak of 'knowing'
religious matters. (C. Barrett, ed., *Lectures and Conversations on
Aesthetics, Psychology and Religious Belief* [Berkeley: University of
California Press, 1967] p. 57 ff.) But we do—or people do—say they
know them, and they are 'ordinary' in the sense of being fairly commonly held and respected. Therefore I think it is a mistake to exclude
them from a general discussion of belief and knowledge.

a person choose the one expression over the other? What point is there in choosing to say one knows rather than believes? Since both express conviction, *there is no difference.* Here the distinction between a strong belief and knowledge has disappeared. If one did pause to 'reflect' on which to say, his hesitation would be hard to interpret.

Again we have failed to find a case that satisfies Prichard's description. We find instead a case that exhibits no contrast between saying one knows and saying one believes. If there is a distinction between knowing and believing, must it not be present here? Can the difference come and go with a change in circumstances? This is an important and unsettling possibility. For we naturally assume that, if two things like knowing and believing are distinct, they are always distinguishable and always in the same way. Prichard surely means to imply this when he writes: "We should only say we know something when we are certain of it, and conversely; . . . on the other hand, when we believe something we are uncertain of it."[7] Prichard implies that whenever we say we know a thing we communicate our certainty and whenever we say we believe a thing we communicate uncertainty. But is this true? What we find by looking at the use of these expressions is that they are sometimes paired in that way and sometimes not. Sometimes there is a contrast between them and sometimes there is none. Then what can be said of *the* distinction between knowing and believing? It is drawn in different ways, more or less sharply, and sometimes not drawn at all. That is what we observe. What is true of one way of drawing it will not be true of another. In this regard Prichard was mistaken.

Someone might object to the Case 2 examples that they involve incorrect uses of 'I know.' For, it might be said, in

7. *Op. cit.*, p. 88. I put to one side the intriguing question how 'I believe' can express uncertainty or lack of belief. However, I return to discuss it in Chapter IV, Section 4. Prichard is right, that 'I believe' often has this meaning, which is the present issue.

such matters as religion or ethics it is inappropriate to say one 'knows.' These matters necessarily concern questions of opinion, and 'know' is only used by hyperbole. Therefore, it can be argued, no party to such a dispute can know, even though he claims to.[8] But I respond that we are looking at the actual use of 'I know,' and the expression is used in such cases as these. A devoutly religious person may assert that he knows there is a God as certainly as he knows anything. To object that he has no scientific evidence is pointless and academic; it cannot serve to discredit his use of 'I know.' That use is common and natural. It would therefore be a mistake to infer that such a speaker doesn't know what he is saying. We should rather infer that a philosophical doctrine which runs against it is too simple. Another way to respond is to say that we do not need to *agree that* the speaker knows in order to acknowledge that his use of 'I know' is correct and well founded in usage. We do not need to judge in addition whether his statement is true. Still another way to answer is: that 'I know' and 'I firmly believe' are interchangeable here cannot be used as an argument that using 'I know' is incorrect. The facts speak otherwise. What is to be inferred is that any distinction between the uses of these two expressions is here being suspended.

Case 3. Imagine you stand in an airport overlooking the runway and remark that the plane to Chicago has now gone. A person overhearing you asks "Is that right—do you *know* that it left?" How do you answer? You reflect for a moment and then answer that you *believe* it left but you aren't sure. This case seems exactly to fit Prichard's remarks about knowing and believing: here one must answer either that he knows or that he only believes. Here, moreover, answers are not similar or different only in degree. And here reflection seems to play a central role.

What is the difference between answering 'I know' here

8. See above, n. 6.

and answering 'I believe'? What is involved? If we imagine that the person asking "Do you know that?" held a ticket for the Chicago plane, we see there might be a great difference in his response to the two answers. On hearing one, he might suddenly stop in his rush down the ramp, turn and go back; to the other he might react by hurrying faster, or asking yet another person if the plane had gone. Here, in contrast to Cases 1 and 2, the distinction is sharp, and heavy emphasis is put on it.

How do you decide whether to say you know or only believe the plane has gone? Reflection enters in, but what is it you reflect upon? Perhaps this: you recall how you watched your friend, bound for Chicago, board a plane exactly similar to the one which just left; you recall how later such a plane taxied down the runway and rose in the air, having been out of your line of vision for only a few seconds. Reflecting on all this you know now which to say. But do you?

It is easy to imagine two people, standing side by side and watching the same events, who answer the question differently. They have identical evidence and experience to reflect on, yet they arrive at different answers. Must we not conclude, then, that the difference between them is subjective, a difference in their attitudes or states? And must we not also suppose that they each determine which state is theirs in the process of reflecting?

Instead of focusing on the observer's state of mind, let us look at the circumstances surrounding the question. If someone asks me, with an urgent tone, whether I know or believe a thing, I infer there is some importance being attached to my answer. I might well ask what importance, what hangs on how I answer. But whether I do or not, I take this question to signal that there are consequences in the offing. That is, if someone asked the question while insisting that nothing depended on my answer—that there was nothing urgent or important about it—they would imply that it is academic. 'Do you know or only believe that?' has no force without some consequences. It loses its meaning to me, and that is to say it doesn't matter which answer I give, just as it didn't matter in Case 2. Without consequences, the seemingly sharp distinction between knowing and believing becomes blurred again. Normally, to answer 'I know' to it is to give assurance, a sort of guarantee. And which answer I give therefore depends upon how much assurance I want to give.[9] That is what I must decide.

This distinction helps to explain why the difference in two persons' answers, on exactly the same evidence, seems to be 'subjective.' A cautious and conservative person will answer unsurely where another kind of person will claim to know for certain. It also helps explain the role of reflection. A person needs to consider this decision in the way one considers giving advice, as having certain consequences and effects for other people. So that while he says lightly that he knows and is sure of a thing, later, when urgency or importance is attached to his saying this, he may well retract. He may say that he is not so sure after all.

The observation that saying 'I know' is like giving a guarantee was first emphasized by John Austin: "When I say 'I know' *I give others my word: I give others my authority for saying that* 'S is P.' "[10] Austin was no doubt thinking of such a case as 3. He could hardly be thinking of cases like 1 or 2. In these latter 'giving one's word' makes no sense. It is unfortunate that Austin, like Prichard and many others, generalizes

---

9. I do not want to exclude the possibility that a man, faced with a tough decision about which to say, might hold a dialogue with himself and decide to risk the consequences on one side after 'assuring himself' that this risk was minimal. But the sense in which he 'assures himself' or 'guarantees' here is plainly attenuated.

10. "Other Minds," reprinted in *Philosophical Papers* (London: Oxford University Press, 1961), p. 67.

from correct observation of *one* kind of case to something incorrect about the use of 'know' in general. *In general,* 'I know' is not used to give a guarantee. Nor *in general* does it stand in this particular relation to 'I believe.' For there is considerable variety within the use of 'know,' as we can plainly see.

Austin views 'I know' as similar to 'I promise' (which he describes as a 'performative').[11] It is a phrase that signals a certain kind of action, he proposes, and the action here is the 'giving of a guarantee.' I think this is a good description of what happens in Case 3. Giving assurance or guaranteeing is something one does and is not, for example, a report on one's state. In Cases 1 and 2, however, it is not clear that there is any action being performed. What the function of 'I know' is in different cases can best be seen by looking at those cases. The phrase functions in a variety of ways; guaranteeing is one of them. That is the most general conclusion our discussion warrants.

Prichard and many others have made the assumption that 'I know' is always contrasted with 'I believe' and always in the same way. This is false. But we should remark an important consequence of this assumption. Since Prichard holds that this distinction is singular and universally applicable wherever we might say either that we know or believe something, he infers that the question, 'Do I know or only believe?' can be raised of any of our opinions or convictions. This assumption is also evident in Descartes's query which of his opinions were mere prejudice and which certain. Both philosophers thought one could ask, 'Do I know or only believe it?' of any opinion and at any time one pleased, and thought that the question would always have a single and obvious sense. However, the actual use of the question shows that this assumption leads to

11. *Ibid.*

an absurdity. For we are to imagine a philosopher asking himself—as if there were important consequences to follow—for a guarantee, an assurance that some belief is right. And we must imagine that when he answers 'I know' he is giving himself assurance, and when he answers 'I only believe' he is withholding it. Here, as sometimes happens in philosophy, the desire to be profound leads to comedy. The philosopher cannot assure himself in this way. And there are no consequences depending on his answer. For he asks the question in circumstances where he is insulated from consequences, perhaps sitting alone as Descartes was, pondering the nature of knowledge. What Prichard thinks can always be done and Descartes thought it necessary for a philosopher to do—that is to reflect and determine the certainty of what we believe—is instead absurd.

The error of taking an ordinary and useful question out of its usual contexts and importing it into an abstract discussion is common in philosophy. That the question is ordinarily useful leads us in philosophy to puzzlement. How *should* one answer Descartes's question? What *do* we really know for certain? Answers to these *should* exist, we think, yet appear not to. It is suddenly extremely difficult to answer a simple question. It requires an unforeseen and unaccountable intellectual effort. How can this happen? The explanation is this. We make an error in taking the question out of the circumstances where it usually functions and asking it abstractly. This is a practice Wittgenstein often warned against. We suppose that questions are paired with answers without regard for context. If something is known for certain, let us identify it here, Descartes seems to say. Now no reader of Descartes imagines that what Descartes is doing is asking himself for a guarantee—that would be a foolish and empty gesture. Rather we think of him as raising a clear and ordinary question in a pure, a 'philosophical' way, which leaves aside accidental and distracting features, including our ordinary concern for consequences. When Descartes raises the question, we are concerned solely with its answer. This view of the question, however, is mistaken. Without the ordinary consequences and the implication that they matter to us, the point of the question has been lost. It is now without force, academic. How it is answered doesn't matter.

3

I turn now to consider briefly two interpretations of Prichard's view, those of Norman Malcolm and Jaakko Hintikka.

From his concern with Prichard's argument, Malcolm is led to draw a sharp distinction between two ordinary senses of 'know'—a strong sense and a weak one. According to this distinction, when I say I know something and mean 'know' in the strong sense, I mean: "There is nothing whatever that could happen in the next moment or the next year that would by me be called *evidence* [that what I say is false]. . . . No future experience or investigation could prove to me that I am mistaken." On the other hand, if I mean that I know in the weak sense, "I do *now* admit that certain future occurrences would disprove [what I say]."[12]

Although this distinction and its defense constitute the most dramatic contribution of his paper, Malcolm intended it first to illuminate what Prichard says. Surely, Malcolm argues, we cannot discover by reflection whether we know a thing or only believe it, because this often depends upon things unconnected with us. Whether I know that there is water in Cascadilla Gorge depends partly on the condition of the gorge, and that is something I cannot discover by reflecting. However, there is something I *can* discover by reflection when I say that I know water is there: "Reflection can make me realize that I am using 'know' in the strong sense rather than the weak one." How does this help us to understand Prichard?

12. *Op. cit.*, pp. 67–68.

It requires Malcolm's further contention that what he calls 'knowledge in the weak sense' is what Prichard would call 'belief.'[13] Therefore his distinction between the strong and weak senses of knowing is equivalent to Prichard's distinction between knowledge and belief, Malcolm believes.

The tenability of Malcolm's distinction between strong and weak senses of 'know' is considered in a later chapter.[14] Here I will be concerned only with the notion of reflection and the bearing of his distinction on Prichard's argument.

Malcolm asserts that Prichard would consider knowing in the weak sense to be the same as believing. If Prichard conceded this, however, it would be a serious mistake on his part. For, as I have explained, the question 'Do I know or only believe?' comes to importance in philosophy because it already has a potent and unambiguous role in ordinary situations. That is to say, the ground of the question's philosophical importance is the importance we attach in everyday situations to whether one will say, when asked, that he knows or that he only believes. Its importance derives from our use of the two expressions—'I know', 'I believe'—and what we make of their contrast. We cannot therefore substitute in the question the terms 'strong sense of know' and 'weak sense of know,' which lack an everyday foundation. If we ask, "Do you know in the strong sense or only in the weak sense?," Prichard's original concern escapes us. Its philosophical force is gone.

This is the chief difficulty I find with Malcolm's account of Prichard's question "Do I know or only believe?" But I find another which is less straightforward, having to do with the notion of reflection. Malcolm speaks of our reflecting not, as Prichard does, on our state, but on our attitude. Prichard's way of speaking of 'states' of knowledge and belief is, as Malcolm remarks, obscure. But Malcolm's references to 'at-

13. *Ibid.*, p. 71.
14. Chapter VII, Section 1.

titudes' creates difficulties equally severe. Malcolm says that when 'know' is used in the strong sense it expresses or conveys a certain attitude, and the object of this attitude is a particular statement, for example, the statement 'There is an ink bottle on the desk' or the statement '5 × 5 = 25.' Therefore, if someone said he 'knew' something in the strong sense we would infer that he was expressing an attitude toward *some statement*, according to Malcolm. But this contention is surely implausible. It is unreasonable to suppose that knowing in the strong sense can only have statements as its objects, and that knowing that 5 × 5 = 25 implies that a statement was made— that 5 × 5 = 25—toward which one expresses an attitude by saying he knows it. The attitude, if an attitude is what is involved here, should have an object that need not have been expressed already, that can be expressed later or not at all. It would seem that Malcolm needs here not the term 'statement' but 'proposition.'

Consider the hypothesis that we have attitudes toward propositions, among them 'knowing in the strong sense.' Do I have an attitude toward the proposition 'I am sitting at my typewriter'? I cannot think what attitude that would be, although I am sitting at my typewriter. I want to ask: "What is the point of asking that? What is at issue? How did that question come up?" For while I have attitudes toward various things, for example, the 1976 election, they are not attitudes toward propositions. Or they don't seem to be. If Malcolm were to explain that, since I cannot imagine being mistaken about sitting here, I therefore have the attitude 'knowing in the strong sense' toward the proposition that I am, it would seem to me that this 'attitude' had been created out of nothing. It would be plainer to say that I sit here and am wide awake.

Malcolm, like Prichard, makes the assumption that one can ask *in vacuo* whether one knows or only believes (knows in the strong or the weak sense). Both suppose that the answer lies there waiting to be given, an answer which might be evinced in any circumstances. But this is not so. If the question is detached from everyday circumstances and asked 'philosophically,' no attitude is there. We reflect, but we find nothing.

Let me offer a further argument against the idea that we usually or generally have attitudes toward propositions, attitudes that stand ready to be inquired about and described. Suppose someone observes a hit-and-run accident and tells his friend, "I'm sure it was a 1971 Chevrolet sedan, though I only saw it for a second." Later he is asked to testify in court under oath. He is asked whether he knows what kind of car it was and can testify to it. He is warned to be careful as his testimony is important. *Now* he says he is not certain that the car was a Chevrolet of that year, but *only thinks* it was.

What has happened here? Has he taken back what he said earlier? Has his attitude changed? Is there reason to think he lied?

Asked whether he knows or only believes something, a person cannot answer that he does both. Asked whether he can testify to something, a person may not answer both that he can and that he cannot. We would find these answers inconsistent. Yet the case I described is not implausible or even unusual. How are we to describe such a person's state of mind? Did his state change? Did reflection show that he was mistaken in his first remark, that is, in his assertion that he knew? Neither of these alternatives is implied, and neither is right. The correct description of the situation is that which he might himself give: when he said he knew, he was not testifying under oath; later, on the witness stand, he was—justifiably—more cautious. In giving this explanation he is not calling attention to different attitudes toward a proposition; he directs our attention to the different circumstances in which his assertion functions. His assertions must be considered in the light of these.

If one persists in asking: "But which is his *real* attitude toward the statement?" I would respond: "Must there be one? Without seeing how one's answer will function, how is one to understand 'attitude' here?" What is your attitude toward '5 × 5 = 25?' might perfectly well be answered 'Indifference,' 'Boredom,' 'I have none.' To answer 'Absolute certainty' is more peculiar than any of these.

Malcolm's inclination to speak of our having an attitude toward a statement is very similar to the inclination to speak of knowing and believing as 'states' associated with different propositions or states of affairs. It represents the same tendency, the tendency to think of knowing or believing as a single relation we have to a single object, whatever you want to call it. But when you see the different ways in which 'I know' functions in different circumstances, that inclination begins to lose its force. And then no state or attitude toward a given 'object' is necessary.

A weaker interpretation can be given of Malcolm's view about reflecting upon our attitudes. It is this: We can reflect upon our assertion that we know a thing and in so doing realize we were using 'know' in its strong or its weak sense. This claim seems to me unobjectionable. It does not imply that, given a different prologue, we might not now be using 'know' in the other sense instead. And it does not require us to have an attitude toward the *proposition*. It is a little doubtful to me whether there really are two senses of 'know' here, but not at all doubtful that 'I know' is used in different ways.

In passing, I remark that there is here a partial answer to the question of the first chapter, the question how we can consistently deny knowing something which was implied by something we said we knew. The explanation must follow the line that in different circumstances the question whether one knows and the assertion that one knows have different implications and force. There is no answer to the question, raised out of the blue, 'Do you know . . . ?'—not because one doesn't know but because the question 'raised out of the blue' is no real question. In circumstances where someone is questioned about the implications of something he said, the effect or force of this may be the same as the effect of 'Do you know or only believe?' And in such a case, a conservative answer is perfectly understandable. As a person does casually things he wouldn't do on a formal occasion, so our remarks about what we know vary with the solemnity of their context. This is only to repeat the truth that using language is part of life's activity, not a routine practiced apart.

I turn now to consider some remarks of Jaakko Hintikka on Prichard's distinction between knowing and believing.[15] Hintikka is interested in how the statement form '*a* knows that he knows that *p*' is related to the statement form '*a* knows that *p*'. The context of this is an attempt to show systematically what relations hold between various 'epistemic' notions. He singles out one sense of 'know' which he calls sometimes the 'strong' sense (following Malcolm) and sometimes the 'fullest sense' or the 'normal sense.' He then represents *all that a person might say he knows on a given occasion* as a set of propositions, some of them connected along the lines of material implication and equivalence. So, for instance, if a person might say that he knew *p* and if it is understood that implies *q*, then inasmuch as '*a* knows that *p*' is in the set, '*a* knows that *q*' must also be. The meaning of 'knows' (and 'believes') is contained in this theory of model sets by virtue of such relations holding; a small number of conditions govern the notions and give rise to formal proofs.

Hintikka asks in this setting how in general the forms '*a* knows that *p*' and '*a* knows that he knows that *p*' are related. By a short proof he shows that if one of them belongs in a given set, so does the other; they are 'virtually equivalent.'[16] This derives from the conditions established for 'know.'

15. *Knowledge and Belief*, pp. 103–123.
16. Pages 104–105.

Hintikka doesn't deny there are other senses of 'know' in which these forms are not equivalent, but claims that they are 'residual' meanings. I will discuss this later.

Hintikka finds himself in agreement with Prichard that where one knows, one also does or can know that one knows. But Hintikka thinks they are equivalent, while Prichard does not. If he thought they were, Prichard would not have so emphasized reflection, which is supposed to show whether one knows or not.[17] It is Prichard's error, Hintikka thinks, to hold that knowing is a state; in contrast, Hintikka holds that 'I know' is "quasi-performative." He explains: "Whoever says 'I know that p' proposes to disregard the possibility that further information would lead him to deny that p although he could perhaps imagine (logically possible) experiences which could do just that.[18] It is true that 'I know' is sometimes performative, and also true that it is unhelpful to call knowing a state. But Hintikka's account contains a number of difficulties.

The chief difficulty has to do with Hintikka's choice of a basic sense of 'know.' Prichard considered knowing to be partly or even largely subjective and therefore considered introspection relevant to determining whether one knows. But for Hintikka, the subjective sense of know is only a 'residual meaning,' and residual meanings of 'know' and 'certain' are not the subject of his analysis.[19] Therefore it is rather surprising that Hintikka treats Prichard's account at all. For, from

17. Pages 109–111.
18. Page 20.
19. He writes: "The multiplicity of residual meanings [of 'a knows that he knows that p'] which I do not claim to have exhausted, may not be entirely unrepresentative of the richness and fluidity of ordinary language. . . . Notice, however, that recognizing this multiplicity has not necessitated any changes in the relatively simple rules which are basic to our study, or diminished their importance" (p. 123). However what one makes of the expression 'a knows that he knows that p' obviously depends on which meaning one takes as the 'full' or 'primary' sense of 'know.'

his approach, he can do little to clarify Prichard's view, and their agreement—or near agreement—on the connection between knowing and knowing that one knows is misleading, since they mean different things by knowing.

Hintikka's reading of ordinary uses is also questionable. Considering the 'residual meanings' which can be given to knowing that one knows, he describes a doctor saying to a patient who is convinced that he has diagnosed his disease, "But do you *know* that you know"? Here Hintikka finds the iterated phrase to have the special effect of indicating that 'knows' is being used in its "fullest sense."[20] It is therefore inside the framework where knowing and knowing that one knows are virtually equivalent. It seems to me more reasonable, however, to interpret that example along the lines of Case 3, that is, as being concerned with whether the patient would risk the consequences in case he is wrong, whether he is quite ready to wager heavily on being right. I am not sure what it is to indicate that 'knows' is being used in the "fullest sense," but I can understand this interpretation. And rather than a 'residual use' of 'know'—one involving some 'special effects'—this Case 3 use seems to me a very important and characteristic one. It is, indeed, the one which many philosophers appear to have wanted to import into philosophical discussions of knowledge. That it cannot be so introduced is one claim; that it is an unimportant or 'residual' use is another—one I would not concede.

Hintikka's description of his approach is revealing. He begins by saying that the meaning of the words 'knows that one knows' is not clear, and that "it would be rash to maintain that they have [in ordinary language] a definite meaning which

20. Although Hintikka's account of the meaning of this, i.e., that "the iteration of the words 'knows that' merely serves to indicate that they are being used in their full sense" (p. 120) differs from mine, I think he would say they both involve "special effects" and are *therefore* "residual meanings" of 'know.'

we are only elucidating by means of our rules and conditions".
Nevertheless he suggests we can approach the question of
what they mean by giving them a definite meaning. This he
does. Armed with a stipulated meaning for the problematic
statements that one knows that one knows a thing, Hintikka
indicates how he can now proceed:

> We may assume, for a moment, that our conditions are correct,
> and see what these problematic statements will turn out to mean
> on this assumption. If we are on the right track, we should then
> be able to explain why these particular types of (putative) state-
> ments are less clear-cut than others, why their meaning easily
> fluctuates. . . . In this way, a study of the pathological cases may
> serve to confirm our analysis.[21]

This approach is clearly circular. The actual uses of the phrase
'knows that one knows'—being insufficiently clear-cut—are
put aside as 'residual' until after Hintikka has shown that, in
the 'primary' or 'fullest' sense of know, 'knowing that one
knows' is roughly equivalent to 'knowing.'

One assumption which is shared by Prichard and Hintikka
accounts for much that is wrong in both accounts. Both assume that there is a single (primary) sense or meaning of
'knowing,' and that by the study of *that meaning*, either by
introspection or model-set analysis, light is shed on the subtler
questions of epistemology. Both attempt to give answers to the
question of what knowing is. Both try to account for the general relation between knowing and believing and that between
knowing and knowing that one knows. But if the meanings of
these phrases shift, and if these shifts are accounted for by the
different circumstances in which remarks are made about
knowing, then both efforts are doomed to failure. There is
no singular state or condition which *is knowing* for a philosopher to introspect on; nor is it possible for Hintikka to prove
that there is a set of sentences which a given person *might say*

21. Page 103.

he 'knows' at a given moment.[22] For the circumstances will shape what 'know' means. To speak of what is known *simpliciter*, unconditionally, must be to leave the actual use of 'know' behind. While Hintikka is right in saying that Prichard cannot introspect knowing because it isn't a state, he is wrong to think that he himself can capture it in the system of model sets. I think he is misled partly by the notion that propositions are connected like wagons or train cars, by rigid hitches, and that these connections are reflected consistently in our assertions about what we know and believe. This misleading idea will be explored in later chapters.

4

The question whether one knows or only believes has been given an important role in the theory of knowledge; it is thought to be one issue which the theory of knowledge clearly is about. We do make a distinction between knowing and believing, and how we do it must be of importance to explaining the nature of knowledge.

As we look closely at this issue, however, we find that 'making the distinction' has itself gone out of focus. What is it to make the distinction? What are we doing when we draw it? What is implied by drawing it? The answers to these questions are: We do different things, imply different things, make it with an eye to different things. Of course that is an unsatisfying result. But it is anyway the right one.

Asking how we ordinarily manage to distinguish knowing a thing from merely believing it does not reveal the shape of the concept of knowledge. It doesn't show us what human knowledge is. But it can lead us to see how we employ that concept in our everyday activities, concerns, and relations with others. Perhaps that is what we should have wanted to

---

22. A different proof of this will be given in Chapter III, Sections 1–3.

know all along. For by now it is clear and plain that the philosophical question 'Do I know or only believe?' is an anomaly.

This discussion of knowing and believing yields an important observation for our future use: we ought to avoid hastily supposing that 'I know that p' and 'I don't know (don't feel sure) that p', because of their contradictory appearances, are inconsistent in actual use. That is to say, it is wrong to suppose that a given person *cannot consistently say both* of these things. For we now see that the force of 'Do you really know that p and not just believe it?' is to encourage a person to be cautious about saying he knows under the shadow of consequences. Remove these and he will more likely than not return to saying he knows. Then are the two inconsistent? I cannot see that they are. Both remarks are useful. They belong to the behavior of a reasonable man. What he is doing is no more inconsistent than his taking a walk to the end of the street, turning and coming back; it is no more inconsistent than accepting money for one debt and then paying it back for another. If a chess piece is moved to a certain position in one part of the game and moved back in a later part, does this reveal an inconsistency? Was the original move 'taken back' or revoked? One has to say that in the changing game both moves may have been right. They do not conflict.

At this point I ask again: what is the role of reflection in deciding to say one knows rather than just believes. Obviously in some cases reflection counts hardly at all. In others, it can be as troubling as a serious moral decision, and never be happily resolved. Can we say, from such cases as these, what is reflected *on?* On the circumstances, on one's situation, on the consequences of the different responses. How do we decide? How do we ever decide what to do? Does this have a general answer? We may explain a decision like this: I considered this fact and that fact in the light of this general rule, and came to the opinion that. . . . That is how I made it. Did I reflect *on my state?* Yes, but that doesn't seem to be the central thing.

Nor is it easy to describe what kind of 'state' I was reflecting on. My decision, for example, to move the queen, may have reflected my feeling bold at that moment; yet it doesn't seem precise to say I reflected *on* my state of boldness.

Now if the reflection I engage in to come to an answer to the question 'Do you know or only believe?' is not reflection on a state but reflection on the circumstances and consequences of the alternative responses, then it seems to me strange to call this sort of reflection 'introspection.' When someone imagines himself pondering what to say when under oath, for example in answer to questions about what he witnessed two months previously on a murky evening, he reflects certainly on the scene, the events that occurred in it, how clear they were, what could have been different without his having noticed, how likely a mistake might be under those circumstances, and so on. It seems to me wrong to call this introspection. What results from it, for one thing, is not the description of a state of mind. What emerges is a description of events, perhaps with qualifications about exactly how they happened. But this description does not result from his studying his *state*. Why then should we be inclined to say it is the state that he was reflecting on? Plainly we should not.

Therefore, I offer another in the series (begun by Malcolm and continued by Hintikka) of backhanded defenses of Prichard's remarks on knowing that one knows. He is correct in saying that, where one answers the (Case 3) question whether one knows or only believes, there is generally or often reflection (as there may not be in other uses of 'know'), and that it plays a very important part in deciding how to answer. Nevertheless, he is wrong in thinking the reflection is introspection. The reflection is not directed to one's state, but to the circumstances or facts as we know them and the nature of the consequences which may attend one's answer. All in all, Prichard is more nearly in touch with the real uses of 'know' and 'believe' than many philosophers, particularly in holding firm to the idea that we do make this distinction in a serious and reflective way, and by insisting that this fact has importance for a philosophical account of knowledge. But he is mistaken in thinking that the question 'Do I know or only believe?' can be employed as a philosophical question. It needs its context, as philosophical questions do not; it cannot be uprooted and brought into the classroom for analysis without the loss of its original—and interesting—character.

III

Examples of What One Knows

> Moore says he *knows* that the earth existed long before his birth. And put like that it seems to be a personal statement about him, even if it is in addition a statement about the physical world. . . . But Moore chooses precisely a case in which we all seem to know the same as he, and without being able to say how. (Ludwig Wittgenstein, *On Certainty*)[1]

In several of his essays, G. E. Moore gave what seem to be examples of things that he knew: 'I am now standing and not sitting down,' 'There are windows in that wall and a door in this one,'[2] 'Here is a hand.'[3] In offering them as examples he implies that, while each one seemed to him clearly to be an example, each might have been replaced by something different without changing the consequences he wished to draw.

1. G. E. M. Anscombe and G. H. von Wright, eds., G. E. M. Anscombe and D. Paul, trans. (New York: Harper, 1969), 84 (numbers here and hereafter refer to numbered sections of the text). Italics are Wittgenstein's.

2. "Certainty," included in *Philosophical Papers* (London: Allen and Unwin, 1959) p. 223.

3. "A Proof of the External World," *op. cit.* p. 144.

Therefore it was not important that Moore choose exactly these examples of things he knew, but it was important that they show transparently the feature which concerned him. It was important that the examples be good ones.

1

Moore certainly thought each of his examples was a good one. He thought that the people he was addressing would see what each of them was an example of and would accept that he knew them. Of course, for his audience to accept that Moore knew each thing he mentioned, it is further necessary that the members of the audience should know or think they know each one as well. That is necessary for Moore's examples to be good ones. So if people doubted or did not know those things Moore said *he* knew, they could not see that Moore's examples were truly examples of things he knew; the examples would fail to show what it was that interested Moore. It follows then that for Moore's examples to be good examples of things he knew, they must be things which the members of Moore's audience knew or thought they knew as well. It might not have been a good example to say that Galileo was tried in 1633, for some in his audience may not have known or ever learned this, and some may have thought it false. If there were such uncertainty about his examples, that would spoil them as examples. It would be similar to Moore's showing his audience something as an example of poor workmanship and some of his audience finding it well made, or to his giving cabbage as an example of uninteresting food when some people thought it delightful. In such cases Moore would want to change his example to something everyone agreed about.

Although this feature of Moore's examples—that they are matters his audience can all be assumed to know—seems necessary for them to be good examples, it has also provoked criticism. Norman Malcolm argued that Moore's examples were not such that Moore could say he *knew* them in any "normal" or "natural" sense of 'know.'[4] Malcolm argues that Moore was really using 'know' in a 'philosophical' way. Normally, Malcolm argues, a person does not say he knows a thing unless the following conditions are present: a doubt exists regarding the thing one claims to know; an investigation exists relating to the matter; and there is some result of the investigation which would settle the doubt.[5] But it follows from Malcolm's description of the normal use of 'I know' that Moore could not possibly give his audience any good examples of things which he 'knew' in a normal sense of 'know.' For a good example would be one the audience accepts without doubt or hesitation; and if Moore gave any example of this sort it would, according to Malcolm, involve an abnormal sense of 'I know.'

Wittgenstein was also among those puzzled by the strange and perfect security of Moore's examples. Propositions like these, he thought, play such a fundamental role in our thinking that to consider doubting or investigating them shakes our very concepts of investigation and proof.[6] Their being in this way 'certain' makes them very strange examples of what anyone knows. There appears to be no alternative to knowing them. Their 'status' is distinctive.

There is something unnatural about Moore's use of 'I know,' as Malcolm says, and this seems (as he says) to derive from the fact that everyone else knows what Moore claims to. We don't normally say that we know something when everyone in hearing can be assumed to know it as well. We don't say, for example, that we know our names, or know that we have two hands unless someone can be supposed to doubt or wonder if we do. Nor do we say of others that they know such things, unless we think it is doubtful *to someone* that they do know. It may be objected that we *might* say such things:

4. "Defending Common Sense," *Philosophical Review*, 58 (May 1949) 201–220.
5. Page 203.
6. See Wittgenstein, *op. cit.* 191–211, 279–80, 369ff, *inter alia*.

for example, if someone's brain had been damaged and we had just discovered that some of his responses are normal, we might say that he now knows his name. But then we have, in giving such an example, provided the assumption that he does not know it. And this assumption is not compatible with Moore's giving good examples of things he knows.

If someone has amnesia, he can say he doesn't remember his name. But if he doesn't have amnesia, he cannot naturally say he remembers it. A person having one arm amputated can say he knows he has only one hand; but someone having the two hands he was born with cannot naturally say he knows he has two. We can imagine in the future saying that we know a person comes from Mars, but cannot imagine saying now that we know our neighbor comes from Earth. What we all know, or think we know, provides awkward examples for Moore of what he knows. But Moore seems to have no other choice.

It seems really paradoxical that knowing something—normally—is like knowing you have only one hand but not like knowing you have two, and like knowing someone is from Mars but not like knowing he is from Earth. It seems paradoxical that knowing should be *un*usual, like forgetting your name, instead of usual, like remembering it. And it seems paradoxical that it should be impossible to give examples of what one knows.[7] The study of examples is an established way of proceeding since Plato. Must we give up this method of studying knowing?

2

I would like to reserve the expression 'I know' for the cases in which it is used in normal linguistic exchange.

7. In a rejoinder to Malcolm's article ("On Speaking with the Vulgar," *Philosophical Review*, 58 [Nov. 1949], 616–621) Max Black took the paradoxical nature of these contrasts as showing that Malcolm's criticism of Moore was in general wrong. I argue that, while Malcolm characterized the use of 'I know' too narrowly, his main thesis was right.

Why doesn't Moore produce as one of the things he knows, for example, that in such-and-such a part of England there is a village called so-and-so? In other words, why doesn't he mention a fact that is known to him and not to *every one* of us? (Ludwig Wittgenstein, *On Certainty*)[8]

Since it has become important how 'know' actually is used and whether there is a use in which Moore can give examples of what he knows, let us consider some ordinary ways in which 'know' functions. We can compare Moore's 'examples' with them to see what (if anything) is wrong.

Case 1. A teacher asks of a class: "Who knows Boyle's law?" ("the population of Bombay?" "the route of Magellan?"). Someone responds that he knows and then he gives his answer. What is the force of 'I know' when he responds? For one thing, it is like a signal, like raising his hand for instance. And what does that signal do? It serves to say that he has learned the answer, learned it and not forgotten. The person who raises his hand is distinguished from the one who does nothing: the person who says he knows is distinguished from someone who remains silent. This is typically the function of 'I know' where students are tested on what they have been told to learn. It is the sense in which a person knows what he has been trained to do. Here 'I know' means roughly: 'I have learned it and not forgotten,' or 'I can do it as I'm supposed to.' One may know a variety of things in this way, first aid and criminal law and calculus, for instance. And the use of 'know' with respect to these reflects nothing more or less than the ability to respond in a certain way. It does not, for example, reflect a degree of certainty or possession of evidence.[9] This is why one can say, in these contexts, 'I think I know,

8. *Op. cit.* 260, 462; italics are Wittgenstein's.
9. That knowing does not always involve being certain has been pointed out by Colin Radford ("Knowledge by Examples," *Analysis*, 27 [Oct. 1966], 1–11), and by Alan White ("Certainty," *Aristotelian Society Supplementary Volume*, 46 [1972], 1–18).

but perhaps I don't.' In this sense 'I know' is connected with training.

Is Moore's use of 'I know' like this? It is not. There was no question which Moore's examples answered. Nothing was asked to which he might respond with the signal: 'I know.' Furthermore, Moore could not mean that he had learned or been trained regarding the things he said he knew. He did not *learn* that here is a hand or that there are windows in this wall or that the world has existed a long time—learned these and not forgotten! Finally, Moore's use of 'I know' cannot have been meant to distinguish himself from others who have not learned; that would go against his examples being good ones.

Suppose Moore had said: "Do you want to know the population of Bombay? Well, *I* know what it is—it is. . . ." That would have been a good use of 'I know' and one rather similar to Case 1. Of course it is appropriate insofar as the person addressed doesn't himself know the population of Bombay. And that means it cannot be used as an example of something Moore knows, for such a listener *doesn't know if Moore knows it*. One may trust he knows it, but that is different. It would be like someone showing me an example of a bad job of wiring, to which I might respond that I believe it if he says so. I accept that it is bad without recognizing it myself. Such an example cannot serve as a good example of what he knows.

Case 2. There is a serious discussion about the right route (the strength of the enemy forces, the patient's condition). Someone says he knows what it is and gives his evidence and his conclusion. On this evidence he says he bases being quite sure (very sure, perfectly sure). What is the force of his 'I know' here? Surely it is: I feel certain and have these reasons for being so. The stronger he judges his evidence to be, the greater his certainty and the more forceful is his 'I know.' He would hardly say here that he knows but has no reasons. Nor would he say his answer had been learned and not forgotten. These features distinguish Case 2 uses of 'I know' from those of Case 1.

Can Moore's use of 'I know' be understood in this way? No. For no one was worried whether there was a hand before Moore announced that he knew it. And Moore did not possess evidence for saying that here is a hand. Similarly he did not have evidence that he was standing up or that there is a door in this wall. He had nothing to present as the basis for his certainty.[10] Lastly, his use of 'I know' cannot be connected with his having evidence that others around him lack, for this would vitiate his 'example.' Moore's use of 'know' must be still different.

Case 3. There is a dispute in progress. In the course of it one party says in exasperation that *he knows* what is the right opinion and leaves. His use of 'I know' is different from the two above; he does not mean he has learned the right answer nor is he willing to give evidence. What does he mean by saying he knows? The meaning of this is: I am through discussing the matter, uninterested in further evidence; my mind is settled. This use of 'I know' seems to transcend that of Case 2. For here the speaker may have the same evidence as those disagreeing with him. His 'I know' does not signal that he possesses evidence but, on the contrary, that his mind is fixed. For him there is no further point in weighing evidence, no point in further investigation or proof.[11]

10. Moore, like many philosophers, thought that a claim to knowledge *should* go hand in hand with a justification. Ironically Moore's favorite and most characteristic 'examples' of what he knew lacked anything resembling a justification. But this fact need not be problematical; there are uses of 'I know' unconnected with justifications, as we see.

11. This sense of 'I know' is rather similar to what Malcolm calls the 'strong sense' of 'know'; however, it cannot be used appropriately in Malcolm's illustrations. Furthermore, this use of 'know' has no corresponding third-person use, while it is not clear that Malcolm's is thus restricted. (See "Knowledge and Belief," reprinted in *Knowledge and Certainty*, especially pp. 66–68.) A discussion of Malcolm's strong sense of 'know' occurs in Chapter VII, below.

Can Moore have meant something like this when he gave his examples? He is satisfied, of course, that here is one hand. But there was no debate about that. What is the issue, then, which he is finished with? If Moore had said, "I know that skepticism is mistaken and that's that!" he would have used 'I know' as it is used in Case 3. And he probably did feel like saying something like this. If he had, we certainly would understand what debate he was showing impatience with. But in the cases of 'Here is a hand' and 'I am now standing up,' we do not. And so we cannot say that his 'I know' functions in the present way.

Case 4. Someone says to his friend, "I know what was said ("what the secret was," "who was elected"), but I won't tell you." In contrast to all the other uses, this use of 'I know' is not accompanied by the disclosure of what is known. It is not accompanied with a presentation of evidence, nor does it mean something has been learned. Indeed, it seems not to mean 'knowing' in the fullest sense. What does it mean? It means that the speaker *can* say or disclose something although he refuses to.

Moore cannot mean he knows in this sense, obviously. He cannot mean that he is able to say something which he will withhold. But there is an interesting implication often drawn from cases like this, an implication I would like to point out.

This use of 'I know' seems to show us an important fact about knowing. It seems to show that knowing is separable from asserting or saying or demonstrating that the thing *is known.* A person may know much, may he not, though he refuses to reveal it? And in that case, knowing should be viewed as internal to the knower. It should be viewed as a personal fact about him like his blood pressure or pulse or temperature, which might never be observed by someone outside. One infers that knowing can be regarded as a personal state; it is what it is, whether anyone asks about or doubts it, whether the knower ever reveals it.

The inference contained here is wrong. This use of 'I know' is very closely connected with saying and with other demonstrations that one knows. To see this, only think of how easy it is to infer, in the absence of such demonstration, that this remark shows that the speaker *doesn't* know. In the absence of a demonstration that one knows, the assertion that one knows wobbles, waiting for support. Knowing but not saying is connected with particular circumstances, where, for instance, revealing what one knows would be inconvenient, indiscreet, impossible; but it is also connected with the circumstances in which a demonstration of that knowledge might be expected. In the latter circumstances knowing something is plainly not a personal matter.

Case 5. There is another use of 'I know' which makes it appear that knowing is a state of a person. It is like this: upon being told something, a person responds by saying, 'I *know* that.' It is to say: you don't need to tell me. Examples might be: "You left the key in the lock"—"I know I did"; "Your car lights are on"—"I know they are"; "You have an appointment at three"—"I know I do." In all these cases, 'I know' rebuts the assumption that one forgot or needs to be told.

This use of 'I know' also seems to imply that knowing goes on inside a person regardless of what he says. Is this, then, the use that fits Moore's examples? If someone had tried to 'remind' Moore that he had his hand in the air and warned him, for example, that he should be careful lest he attract unwanted attention or be thought saluting, then Moore might have replied quite impatiently that he *knew* his hand was in the air—it was there because he was giving a philosophical demonstration! That is, in these circumstances one can understand perfectly such a remark as 'I know here is my hand.' But Moore said this without any provocation; he said it without a context that makes it understandable. Can he infer that, since it *would have been* correct to say he knows *had someone reminded him*, therefore it is correct without the reminding? But how are we to understand it? As impatient? As rebutting the assumption that he needed reminding? What assumption? Just as Moore's impatience, as he delivered the sentence 'Here is a hand,' would have been inappropriate and incomprehensible, so the supposition that this remark was meant to rebut the assumption that he didn't know is also incomprehensible. There is no indication such an assumption was being made. There is nothing to rebut.

We began by asking how 'I know' functions in various settings, and we have seen a number of different ways it does. Yet none of them fits Moore's use of 'I know' in giving examples. In giving examples Moore lacks the background that provides a function and sense to saying one knows. In his lecture the context is sterile of clues as to what 'I know' might mean. What is the meaning of Moore's 'I know?' I do not see how we can answer. Malcolm says it is a 'philosophical use.' But what does this mean? If a 'philosophical use' is just one in which a philosopher may give examples, then the issue is whether there is such a use. What is at issue is whether it makes sense to proceed as Moore does.

It may be objected: but we can surely consider whether Moore knew what he asserted he knew, and in that case we can discover whether his instances or examples are really examples of what he knew. If they are, then in some sense, Moore's use of 'I know' and his giving examples is vindicated. The answer is that we do not know what force there was to Moore's assertion, and therefore we don't know what the question 'Does Moore know as he says or not'? amounts to. Nor can we see even one way to interpret this question so that it clearly relates to Moore standing in the lecture hall and addressing persons who have no doubt and no interest in the things he declares he knows—to Moore addressing persons who have not raised questions about or debated the things

Moore says he 'knows,' nor implied that Moore did not know any of them. What is the answer to, "Did Moore know?"[12] One wants to say, "The answer must be, *yes, he knew,* for otherwise the answer must be that *he didn't know,* and that's absurd." But the answer to what question? If there is no question, then we don't have to choose between two possible answers. *To no question there is no answer.* We cannot say, "But suppose the question had a clear meaning—then the answer to it would be yes." Again we don't know what meaning it would have. We want to say Moore knows, but we don't want to say what this means—a hopeless position.

3

Philosophers have often thought a catalog could be made up of all that people know. And some have thought that it is one of the jobs of philosophy to consider what is on this list.[13] If there were such a list, then it would be plausible that one could choose examples from it. If there were a list for one person, there could be lists for each person, and then a list possibly comprising what all knew in common. When Moore gives examples of what he knows, he seems to draw from such a list. We need to ask, is there one?

In his notes Moore once proposed to define a "declarative sentence" as follows: "an *English* sentence will be 'declarative' if and only if it *either* (1) begins with 'I know that' or 'I think that' and makes sense, *or* (2) is such that when it is

12. Wittgenstein said, "We just do not see how very specialized the use of 'I know' is" (*op. cit.,* 11). That is the case here.

13. Moore once said in his lectures that "in the case of human knowledge philosophers have tried, and it is their business to try (1) to give an exhaustive list of *kinds* of props. we know for certain, (2) in the case of any kind, with regard to which they conclude we *do* know, to raise the question: How do we know?, and I *might* have added (3) attempt to give an exhaustive list of the *ways* in which we know things" (C. Lewy, ed., *Lectures on Philosophy* [London: Humanities Press, 1966], p. 189).

immediately preceded *either* by 'I know that' *or* 'I think that' the whole makes sense."[14] Moore emends this definition slightly, but does not waver in the main point: certain sentences—a certain class of sentences—are characterized by being the sort of sentence which might be prefaced by 'I know that' or 'I think that.' Put differently, what such sentences assert is something that can be known or believed.[15] If there were such a class or sort of sentences, this would contradict much that I have argued in Chapters I and II. For it would imply that a sentence *per se* is qualified to be appropriately prefaced by 'I know,' without consideration of the circumstances in which this might be said. The meaningfulness of knowing a thing would derive from the object or thing said to be known and from nothing else.

Moore's statement is only one expression of the 'catalog hypothesis,' the hypothesis that there is a kind of thing which is an object of knowledge, and that what one (someone, anyone, everyone) actually knows is a subclass of this class. If such a class of objects can be conceived, the class of things known can be conceived as well.

Are there such classes as these? Is there a class of things which a particular person knows? How would such a list be constituted? Perhaps in the following way: it would include all that one knows as in Case 1 (i.e. what one has learned but not forgotten), and all that one knows as in Case 2 (i.e. everything one knows on the ground of firm evidence), and also whatever one is fixed about and uninterested in discussing (after the manner of Case 3), and all that one is unwilling

14. *Commonplace Book: 1919–1953* (London: Allen and Unwin, 1962), pp. 357–358.

15. Among the more recent versions of such a view is one given by Peter Klein, "A Proposed Definition of Propositional Knowledge," *Journal of Philosophy*, 68 (Aug. 1971), 471–482. He writes: "By 'an epistemological theory' I mean a set of beliefs concerning the types of propositions that can (or cannot) be known" (p. 471).

though able to assert truly (like those of Case 4), and all that one would object to being reminded of (similar to Case 5). The combined list would have enormous variety. Items would change in it according as the things one might be reminded of, the things one might be keeping secret, the things one is impatient of discussing, change, which is to say quite often. It would one day include my dentist's appointment and the next day not; one day include my view of telephone war taxes and the next day not. One can hardly imagine such a list having any philosophical importance.

But there is a deeper difficulty than this. If the force of 'know' in each separate item draws its meaning from the context in which it occurs, then one needs a context for including in the list that one knows (having proof) that raccoons have been in the yard, and a context for asserting that one knows (and is finished debating) that auto mechanics are crooks, and that one knows (not needing to be reminded) when it's time for the bus. But these contexts plainly cannot coexist! In drawing up a list, moreover, we are *in the context of drawing up a list*, which is quite different from waiting for a bus or discussing repair bills or considering how the trash got spilled. The contexts necessary for understanding the items on the list will, most of them, be necessarily absent. And what then can be said of their meaning?

It may appear that I am denying that we can speak about such things as 'all that science has discovered,' which includes chemistry, physics, biology, and other sciences, together with their laws and the evidence for them. But I am not denying this. I only argue that this list is also specialized. The sense in which most of us 'know' truths of chemistry is different from that in which we know what's in the basement cupboard and again from that in which we know (having been unnecessarily reminded) that guests are coming to dinner. If we should learn now that some "fact" we learned in chemistry years ago is false, we should not count it our error. We accepted and do accept such information on authority; the logic of 'knowing' it is different from the logic of knowing matter we don't learn this way. 'Everything science has discovered' is learned by us and known in a particular way. We cannot make it the model for a list containing everything we know. A further proviso would be needed even to construct this scientific list: it would be necessary to specify whether the things are known in the manner of scientists who actually verify and apply them or in the manner those of us who know them on authority. For the function of 'know' will differ accordingly.

The difficulty of drawing up a list of everything we—or particular persons—know results from there being no generic, context-independent sense of 'know.' We are driven at each turning to speak of a particular sense of knowing; but specifying a particular sense plainly makes the list of all that we know impossible. The requirement of a kind of knowing which is knowing *simpliciter*, on which Moore's examples depend, is just what is required for a list of all we know. And if there is no such sense, then it is futile to try to give either the list or the examples.

Would it not be possible to speak of such knowing for philosophical purposes only? Have we not the option of putting forward a generic sense of 'know'? Then we could speak of both the list and examples. But our list and examples would not then be drawn from what we ordinarily claim to know. They would be artifacts produced by practicing philosophy in a certain way; we would have no ground to think such a list represented a list of everything we ordinarily know.

Isn't there a sense to 'what we all know'? Of course! It appears when for example a speaker says, "We all know there is corruption in high places in government," or a teacher says, "We all know that the prevailing winds are easterly." But these actual uses are rhetorical. They would not serve as

paradigms for making a list or giving examples as Moore
wanted. We have run again into specialized functions of
'know.'

The desired list of what we all know is a philosophical list.
It is a philosophical goal, just as it is a philosophical goal to
give good examples of what we know. These goals require a
philosophical sense of 'know,' one that does not exist in the
ordinary use of language. However, if philosophers need such
a special sense of 'know' to study knowledge, it can be inferred that the way they are studying knowledge is wrong.

4

This argument runs crosswise to our intuitions about
knowledge. Why is it we can speak of an example of something learned, for example by a child on a nature hike, but
not of an example of something he knows? That seems paradoxical. What one has learned and not forgotten one *knows*.
Context seems irrelevant; having learned and not forgotten, it
follows that one knows. Furthermore, it is possible to give
examples of scientific facts and discoveries which have been
learned and are now known. Therefore there must be examples of what we know, and we must be able to find them.
Without them, there would be no sum total of scientific truth,
no textbooks presenting it, and no sense to 'extending it' by
further investigations. All these ways of speaking point directly to the existence of a sum total of knowledge, a collection of all that we know. If our own language leads us this
way, how can we be led wrong?

Let us look at the question sometimes put to a child: "What
did you learn today?" Possible answers would be: "I learned
to play ball", "I learned the nine timeses," "I learned not to
talk in class." These are all good enough answers. And each
means that something is now known which was not known
before today. Each could be viewed as an example of what
was learned today. Why is it not a straightforward enlarge-

ment of this question to ask what he has learned *simpliciter*? Let us imagine asking a child to give us an example of something he has learned. Would he not react with puzzlement, baffled at what we mean? "When?" he might respond, or "What do you have in mind?" The bigger question is obscure, though the narrow one was not. Would it be satisfactory for him to answer that he has learned to eat with a fork, to say "please" when asking for something, that 25×25 is 625, to keep quiet in class, to mimic his teacher? That all these have a home in one class is hard to accept. The reason why the larger question is obscure is just that there is no required class. There is no class of things learned *simpliciter* just as there is no class of things known *simpliciter*. We can relate what we learned in Biology I, or what happened today, or what was overheard while waiting for the train. But we cannot look at our entire experience in this way. We cannot examine or enumerate the entire contents of our mind.

We nevertheless resist this idea. Do we not speak of a person possessing knowledge, and having enough knowledge? Do we not say that someone trained has knowledge, which someone untrained lacks? Do we not speak of learning as the acquisition of knowledge? All these ways of speaking show that knowledge is acquired, that more may be acquired or less, and the total for one person may exceed that for another. How shall we hold a view consistent with these ordinary truths unless we hold that knowledge comprises a class? To say that these phrases are mere metaphors is unconvincing. They are so numerous and harmoniously used, they cannot be viewed as aberrations or as unusual and especially vivid ways of speaking. The objection is not to be dismissed by calling these phrases figures of speech. But then do they show us a philosophical truth? Does it follow from our use of these expressions that we should be able to speak of a class of all the things we learn? Does it follow that knowledge, like physical possessions, admits of inventory?

It is an ancient and powerful temptation to think of what is known as a collection of things. 'Knowledge' is viewed as a concept under which instances fall just as individual zebras fall under the concept 'zebra.' Your knowledge is possessed by you like your shoes and socks, and mine is possessed by me. Plato gave us a wonderful image to this effect:

Let us now suppose that in the mind of each man there is an aviary of all sorts of birds—some flocking together apart from the rest, others in small groups, others solitary, flying anywhere and everywhere.

He applies the image:

We may suppose that the birds are kinds of knowledge, and that when we were children, this receptacle was empty; whenever a man has gotten and detained in this enclosure a kind of knowledge, he may be said to have learned or discovered the thing which is the subject of the knowledge: and this is to know.[16]

Knowing is understood here as the possession of objects, and the objects are what is known. Under this image, what one knows is conceived as a class of such objects.

Elsewhere in the *Theaetetus* Plato puts forward the premise: 'All things and everything are known or not known,' and he compares the objects of thought with the objects of vision and hearing,[17] things separate but of one class. In the *Meno* too he speaks of "a single recollection" out of the class of things once known.[18] Throughout his thinking about knowledge, the image of a class of objects recurs and shapes the argument. Without this in mind one cannot follow his thought.

This image is very pervasive in philosophy. Descartes wrote about "all the thoughts and conceptions . . . that ever en-

16. *Theaetetus*, Steph. 197, II, p. 202.
17. *Ibid.*, Steph. 188, 189, II, pp. 191–192.
18. *Meno*, Steph. 81, I, p. 360.

tered into my mind,"[19] and of "all that up to the present time I have accepted as most true and certain," and of "the general upheaval of all my former opinions".[20] We are brought constantly to look at knowledge as a subclass of our opinions, and it never troubles Descartes whether there *can* be classes of these two kinds. It does not surprise us, then to find him writing in the same vein that many philosophers were to write in subsequently: "For example, there is the fact that I am here, seated by the fire, attired in a dressing gown, having this paper in my hands."[21] Where there is a collection, how can there be a difficulty in picking out one member to serve as an example?

The conviction that what we know comprises a class has been more universal than any view about what kind of object falls in it. Thus Locke defines 'idea' relatively to thought. It is "that term which, I think, serves best to stand for whatsoever is the *object* of the understanding when a man thinks."[22] These objects are the "furniture" of the mind,[23] the things "painted" on the white paper of the infant mind, the "materials" of reason and knowledge.[24] I believe what gives rise to these figures of speech is the primary assumption that what we know is a collection. The need to talk about individual 'objects' in that collection follows directly.

A similar pattern can be found in Hume, who speaks of "all the objects of human reason or enquiry."[25] It is also common

19. "Discourse on Method," (*The Philosophical Works of Descartes*, E. Haldane and G. R. T. Ross, trans. (Cambridge: Cambridge University Press, 1967), I, 101.

20. *Meditations*, Descartes, *op. cit.* I, 144.

21. *Ibid.*, p. 145.

22. *An Essay Concerning Human Understanding* (New York: World, 1964), p. 66. The italics are Locke's.

23. *Ibid.* The phrase "furnish the mind" occurs frequently throughout Book II, Chap. 1.

24. *Ibid.*, p. 89.

25. *An Enquiry Concerning Human Understanding*, Sec. III, p. 25.

in the writing of Bertrand Russell, who speaks of the "data" which we begin with in the philosophy of knowledge, and then the "extension" of this data and eventually its systematization. He tells us that there are "varying degree(s) of certainty attaching to different data" and speaks of the "vague, complex, inexact body of knowledge which it is the business of the philosopher to analyze."[26] Throughout we have standing behind these phrases the image of knowledge as a class or collection which must then be understood to be a collection *of objects*. What the objects *are* is more difficult to understand than that they must exist.

A common recent interpretation of the objects of knowledge has been that they are propositions; then of course the class of things known would be a class of propositions. Roderick Chisholm, for example, gives this definition of knowledge: "S knows that *h* is true" means: (i) S accepts *h*; (ii) S has adequate evidence for *h*; and (iii) *h* is true."[27] Jaakko Hintikka follows a similar course in developing his model-sets interpretation, with an interesting variation. Hintikka not only uses 'know' to mean 'knows some proposition *p*,' but also defines 'all that one knows' to consist in the set of statements which a person might assert that he knows at some particular time. Assuming that there is such a set, he finds it simple to define 'consistency' for it:

The consistency of a set of sentences will only mean that, whenever this set of sentences is uttered (on one and the same occasion by one and the same speaker or writer, addressed to one and the same person, and so forth) then the resulting set of statements is consistent in so far as one can tell without knowing who the speaker is, when the statements were made, or any other facts about them except the forms of words they exemplify.[28]

26. *The Problems of Philosophy* (London: Oxford University Press, 1959), pp. 72, 75.
27. *Perceiving* (Ithaca, N.Y.: Cornell University Press, 1957), p. 16.
28. *Knowledge and Belief*, p. 8.

What is the connection between this set and what we say we know? There is no occasion for asserting such a set, nor, as I argue, do the various uses of 'know' permit that there might be such an occasion. The entire scheme is based squarely on a fiction, an imaginary picture of knowing. Its justification is that we use phrases about 'all we know' and 'what we all know'; these lead one to the conclusion that there must be such sets of things. But this is a fragile basis for large conclusions about the nature of knowledge.[29]

What Hintikka's theory shows us is how epistemic terms might be connected if what one knows were a class of propositions. And what Chisholm defines is a relation between a person and a proposition, but not a relation that has any claim to the term 'knowledge.'

I am proposing that 'knowledge' is not a class concept. There is not a class of things known or a class of things knowable. Birds in a cage is a fine metaphor, but how should we interpret the 'birds'? Philosophers have puzzled a good deal about this, and supposing they are propositions is only the last in a series of inadequate interpretations. The difficulty does not stem from the notion of proposition any more than from Plato's confusion about the birds. It comes from the false but attractive assumption that what we know is a collection of things.

Much the same is true of the notoriously difficult term 'idea.' Its introduction and its obscurity arise from an assumption, an image, a prejudice, which philosophers can neither shake off nor bring into critical focus: the assumption that there is a class of things one knows. Moore's position in this

29. Alan White's valuable paper "What We Believe" (included in the American Philosophical Quarterly monograph No. 6, *Studies in the Philosophy of Mind* [Oxford: Blackwell, 1972] presents several powerful objections to the idea that only a particular kind of object serves as an 'object of belief.' Many of the same considerations apply to 'objects of knowledge.'

tradition explains his incorrect view of examples of what one knows.

How did Moore, who was so exacting in his observations about language, come to adopt this assumption? As we have seen, it is not difficult to find phrases in common use which suggest it. Furthermore, 'know' is a transitive verb, and so grammatically always has an object. What is more natural than to suppose that all the objects or possible objects of knowledge form a class?[30] But this inference represents the not uncommon mistake of supposing that language accurately describes its own workings. That is, it supposes that language tells us how its concepts are to be described (for example, by such phrases as 'all that one knows'). But to suppose that is to misunderstand the relation of philosophy to language. These phrases too have their ordinary use: they do not carry philosophic weight. It is left to a philosopher to observe and describe how 'know' works without being influenced by such phrases. And what he finds is this: we know a vast assortment of things—names and how to do things and lines of poetry and mathematics and polite behavior. Nothing suggests that they form one class, neither their similarities nor our talk about them. And indeed the use of 'know' dictates that such a class cannot exist.

We now better understand the paradox with which we began—that we can naturally say we know we have one hand but not that we have two; that we can say we know someone comes from Mars but not that someone comes from Earth. The paradox stems from the assumption that we must know the very familiar things of our lives and surroundings, for otherwise they would fall outside the class of things we know. And this in turn rests on the assumption that there is such a class.

It is sometimes argued that it is a mistake to concentrate so

30. My own use of the tiresome words 'thing' and 'something' has been dictated by the need for grammatical objects where no legitimate objects exist; to be more precise than this would be to err.

much on what we actually say, for what we say only shows what we have occasion to remark upon.[31] Countless things are assumed and known which are never mentioned, and nothing can be more certain than these. Although this view will be treated under the subject of truisms later, it is useful to discuss one version of the objection briefly here. John Searle argues that it is a mistake to look constantly to the *use* of such expressions as 'know' and 'remember' in order to describe the concepts of knowledge and memory. For in so doing we ask when we would *make assertions*, for example, of the form 'I know that so and so': "But then there is no easy way to tell how much the answers to these questions depend on what it is to *make assertions* and how much is due to the concepts the philosopher is trying to analyze."[32] A devotion to what one can naturally say misleads a philosopher who, noticing that it would be "very odd or bizarre to say certain things in certain situations . . . concludes for that reason that certain concepts are inapplicable to such situations." Searle insists that a concept may be *applicable* even when it cannot sensibly be applied, that is, in an assertion. Meaning concerns the conditions of applicability, which he argues are different from the conditions of assertion.[33]

It is true that I have attended to ways in which we use 'I know.' Only in this way could I have found the rich variety of its uses. Have I then neglected 'the range of the concept's applicability'?[34] This question suggests that the concept stands behind language and is only partially revealed in it, a notion

31. John Searle puts forward the slogan "No remark without remarkableness" to account for the pointlessness of saying, e.g., that I remember my own name, in most normal situations, (*Speech Acts* [Cambridge: Cambridge University Press, 1970], p. 144).

32. *Ibid.*, p. 141. The italics are Searle's.

33. *Ibid.*, p. 147.

34. My own account of asserting in Chapter IV binds it to meaning in a way which further illuminates the nature of language and the puzzles before us here.

invoking as much mystery as Plato's forms. That we don't say, for example, that we know that we have two hands reflects one characteristic of knowing. I cannot see why one would want to say this *doesn't* represent the concept unless he has an argument which leads him to think that *we must know* that we have two hands. And I have tried to show that this view comes from a misunderstanding about how 'know' works and is applied.

Another objection to my argument is this: that argument has not proved that there is no sense of 'know' in which Moore might give examples, but only that I cannot find one. It might seem that I have left the door open to there *being* such a sense, therefore. My response is that I have put the burden of proof on the other side; it is to a defender of examples of knowing to show what sense of 'know' can be employed, to show how that sense works in ordinary, unphilosophical contexts. Just as the end of a chess game comes, not when someone's king is removed from the board, but only when it cannot be moved out of check, so my argument purports to show that the position of the other side is untenable. I show that there are a number of moves he cannot make. I argue that among them is the proposal that there is a generic and philosophical use of 'know' which has no ordinary applications. And without such a sense, it seems clear to me he cannot provide any.

It is true that I wish to draw some general conclusions about knowing, the principal ones being these: There is no way of giving in philosophy a good example of what we know. To give such an example we need a sense of knowing *simpliciter*—knowing regardless of the circumstances and regardless of the force which saying one knows might have in these circumstances. I argue that the use of a sentence beginning with 'I know' changes with the circumstances in which it is asserted. 'Know' is not a concept with a single face, but many, each related to some kind or kinds of circumstances.

Whether we say it is a single concept or a family of fragments does not seem very important.

We cannot proceed in studying the concept of 'knowledge' by giving and studying examples of what we know. Attempting to do so distorts our subject, the matter at hand, for the features that make an example a good one conflict with the features that make the use of 'know' natural. As Wittgenstein said, 'I know' has specialized functions, and to inquire about or assert something as known is to have some one of these functions in mind. As we found in the preceding chapter, the question whether someone knows a thing may have different answers as one imagines a change in contexts, although the person's state and the truth of the thing are held constant. Knowing, by this sign, cannot be construed as a relation holding between a person and an object.

Among the factors contributing to our desire to speak of examples are a number of common phrases suggesting that what one knows is a class of things—phrases like 'whatever one knows,' 'all that one knows,' and so on. We are inclined to think these represent or indicate how 'know' works, and what they suggest to us is that what we know is a class. But these phrases need to be seen as having their own and distinctive uses. They do not depend on other senses or uses of 'know,' nor do they imply that there is a generic sense spreading like an umbrella over the others. Taken descriptively these phrases misrepresent knowing as much as it would misrepresent the movements of a football player to describe them in terms of a dance. The purpose and function of the player, depending as they do on the context, have been left out. You could not understand his movements in this way.[35]

35. Something like this may have been meant by Wittgenstein when he spoke about the difference between 'depth' and 'surface' grammar, for here the indications of the forms of language mislead us about how phrases actually function. We should not expect language to represent its own workings, to be self-descriptive.

There is not for an individual or for humanity a collection of things known. There is no sense of 'know' in which such a totality could be expressed. If we are led to think there must be, because there is one meaning which 'know' has and according to it we either know something or don't, we are misunderstanding how varied and multiform the concept of knowing is. It does not reduce to a singular meaning.

It may seem at this point that we cannot do philosophy the way we want. But in the face of this conclusion it would be a mistake to invent a sense of 'know' which conforms to our desire.

IV

Expressing Beliefs

Moore maintained against Charles Stevenson that the meaning of an ethical judgment does not consist, or even partly consist, in the approval a speaker expresses. It is not part of the meaning of '*x* is right' that a speaker approves of *x*, even though in saying that *x* is right the speaker shows that he approves of *x*. Moore drew this analogy with nonethical judgments:

If, for instance, I assert, on a particular day, that I went to the pictures the preceding Tuesday, I *imply*, by asserting this, that at the time of speaking, I believe or know that I did, though I do not *say* that I believe or know it. But in this case, it is quite clear that this, which I *imply*, is no part of what I assert; since, if it were, then in order to discover whether I did go to the pictures that Tuesday, a man would need to discover whether, when I said I did, I believed or knew that I did, which is clearly not the case.[1]

A person who says that he went to the pictures last Tuesday

1. "A Reply to My Critics," in P. Schilpp, ed., *The Philosophy of G. E. Moore* (New York: Tudor, 1952), p. 541.

implies that he believes he went, although he doesn't say this. Since he doesn't say it, it is not part of the meaning of what he says. Similarly, when someone says that an action is right he *implies,* though he doesn't say, that he approves of the action. Again it is not even part of the meaning of what he says that he approves the action. Stevenson had argued that the connection between approving the action and judging it right is so intimate as to be one of meaning; Moore is arguing that the connection is distinctive and different, since it does not concern what is said.[2]

The connection between our beliefs and what we say gives rise to a paradox: although it may be true that a person went to the pictures and doesn't believe he did, he cannot assert this. He cannot be understood if he says 'I went to the pictures but I don't believe that I did.' Similarly, a person cannot be understood who says 'That action was right, but I don't approve of it.' The obscurity—Moore says the 'absurdity'—of such utterances comes from the fact that we imply more than we say. When we deny a thing we have implied, the result is absurd.

The issue in dispute between Moore and Stevenson arises from differences in their views about meaning. They do not disagree that a connection between attitudes and ethical judgments exists, but they disagree about how to interpret it. This general issue of meaning is the framework for my discussion.

Moore argues that '*x* is right' does not say the same thing as 'I approve of *x*,' for the one can plainly be true when the other is false. If their meanings were the same, they would say the same thing and be true or false together. This conception of meaning is closely related to the practices of giving definitions and translations, two practices that interested Moore in many other connections.[3] The giving of a definition,

2. C. L. Stevenson, *Ethics and Language* (New Haven: Yale University Press, 1944), esp. Ch. 2.

3. E.g., in the *Commonplace Book,* in connection with the nature of philosophical analysis (pp. 365–369); in remarks on sentences and

for instance, is the giving of an expression which purportedly says the same thing as the expression defined; and the sole and sufficient reason for saying that a definition is good is that it provides an expression that says exactly the same thing as the expression being defined.

This notion of meaning is fairly clear. But the new and original notion of 'implication' which Moore introduces is not. How does the implication that a speaker believes something issue from his saying something, but not from the thing he says? Moore explains:

> That you do imply this proposition about your present attitude, although it is not implied by (i.e. does not follow from) *what* you assert, simply arises from the fact, which we all learn by experience, that in the immense majority of cases a man who makes such an assertion as this does believe or know what he asserts: lying, though common enough, is vastly exceptional. And this is why to say such a thing as "I went to the pictures last Tuesday, but I don't believe that I did" is a perfectly absurd thing to say, although *what* is asserted is something which is perfectly possible logically: it is perfectly possible that you did go to the pictures and yet do not believe that you did—that you believe you did does not follow from the fact that you did.[4]

This explanation of implying is unsatisfactory. A person may know that "the immense majority" of people drive on the right-hand side of the road, but he doesn't 'imply' by taking his car out that he will do this. And if he doesn't, you would not call it 'absurd' of him to drive on the left. Depending upon where he is, it may be unconventional, eccentric, dangerous,

---

propositions (pp. 359–361); in connection with the concepts 'true' and 'fact' (p. 319); in his remarks on definitions (pp. 309–315); and in connection with substantives and adjectives (pp. 22–24). Moore, like Russell, thought it was part of the business of philosophy to give careful explanatory equivalents of problematic notions wherever possible.

4. "A Reply to My Critics," pp. 542–543.

but not absurd. Moore fails to explain the striking, the utter incoherence, of the sentence 'I went to the pictures, but I don't believe that I did.' He fails to explain why on the one hand we want to say it must be meaningful because it might be true, and on the other hand we want to say it is not only 'absurd' but *meaningless*. Furthermore, Moore's explanation rests on the notion of truth-telling. But is it too only a convention, a customary practice?

Moore's notion of 'implying by saying' raises a number of questions. It will be my object to show that the 'absurdity' of Moore's example can only be explained by giving an account of the meaning of such sentences very different from Moore's. On this account the nature of the 'absurd' sentence will become clear, and the importance of truth-telling will be seen as more than conventional.

1

The paradox concerning belief and approval was not an isolated concern of Moore's. It was part of a wide interest in the relation that exists between a speaker and the things he says. Moore was intrigued by the question: what is needed to make an assertive form of utterance an assertion? What is missing when a parrot, rather than a person, utters a sentence—for example, 'My name is Nancy'?[5] At one point, Moore inclined toward saying that the difference consists in the speaker's understanding or 'attaching a meaning to' the sentence.[6] But while this seems to explain the difference between a parrot's utterance and a human's, it does not distinguish assertion from other uses of a given sentence. For instance, someone can 'attach a meaning' to a sentence he reads aloud, but it would not follow from this that he is asserting it. Besides attaching a meaning, perhaps a certain intention is

5. *Commonplace Book*, pp. 306–307.
6. *Ibid.*, p. 179ff.

necessary—an intention to convey a certain thing. But this condition is too strong. Moore explains:

If by a slip you say "Broad" when you mean "Moore" you can be said to have asserted that Broad lectured for 4 years at Columbia, when all you intended to assert was that Moore did; & you *can* be said to have *told* people that Broad did.[7]

From this it would appear that our words carry their meaning without anything being added by our saying them. And this brings us back to the parrot. The connection between uttering and asserting seems now even more mysterious.

The paradox about belief arises because it seems to us that we can *see* a sentence's meaning on its face, apart from whether it is or might be asserted. Other paradoxes arising from the same source concerned Moore, the 'liar' and the 'Empimenides' among them. The sentence, 'This sentence is false' is plainly meaningful, and therefore will be meaningful 'in all cases,' Moore infers—which would seem to entail that it is always and unequivocally true or false.[8] But if the word 'this' has no other sentence as its reference, 'This sentence is false' becomes neither true nor false, and therefore apparently meaningless. Similarly the sentence 'All Cretans are liars' is meaningful; yet it cannot be asserted by a Cretan:[9]

A statement, which might possibly have been true, if made by anyone but a Cretan, cannot possibly be true, if made by a Cretan. Or, to put the paradox in a different way: that, if it were true that every statement, without exception, made by a Cretan is false, it would be impossible that any Cretan should ever make this statement. Isn't it strange, perhaps incredible, that there should be any statement whatever, such that from the supposition that it is

7. *Ibid.*, pp. 303–304.
8. *Ibid.*, pp. 170–172.
9. Elsie Myers Stainton remarks that the sentence *can* be used by a Cretan as an excuse for his lying; this observation raises issues regarding the connection between meaning and truth that are treated below.

true, it follows that it is impossible that any person of a particular class should assert the proposition?[10]

This is strikingly similar to the situation with belief and approval: it seems as if we cannot say what others may say meaningfully about us, and what may well be true. It is meaningful to say and it may be true that *x* is right and I disapprove of it; it is meaningful to say and it may be true that I went to the pictures but don't now believe I did. Yet neither of these things can be asserted by me. The central issue in all these paradoxes is the relation of a meaningful sentence to its meaningful—non-absurd—use.

It is plausible to say that we see the meaning of a sentence on its face. We can see what a sentence says and perhaps give an exact equivalent in the same or a different language. We understand it even though we have never had occasion to use it, nor ever observed it being used. We understand sentences like 'I am walking on the planet Mars,' and 'There go three unicorns,' though we have never asserted them and never expect to. These are strong and persuasive reasons for saying that meaning belongs primarily to sentences, for saying that meaning is not something added or taken away or affected by a speaker who utters them.

A very rough idea of what this implies for a theory of meaning can be presented as follows.[11] On this view, learning a language is principally learning when and where certain things are true and truly said. As one learns the names of objects by being taught to sort them, and color words by sorting color chips, one also learns to correlate a sentence with a situation. Once the correlation is learned, the meaning is understood and the use is mastered. Thus, we know what situation 'There go three unicorns' is correlated with. We could identify the picture which represents that situation. The situa-

10. *Commonplace Book*, p. 379.
11. A fuller discussion of this theory is given below in Section 2.

tion never occurs, of course, and this is the reason we don't use—though we understand—that sentence.

This view of the meaning of declarative sentences I will call the 'package' theory. According to it, a sentence carries its meaning within it. In learning to understand it we learn when and when not to send it out, like a package ready to post. The contents are there and they remain what they are whether the package gets sent or not. The meaning of a sentence, on this view, is detached from us. We use sentences, but we do so in something like the way we use forks and books and tools: we can use them because they are independent of us and our purposes.

This is the view of meaning which appears to dominate many of Moore's discussions of propositions, and it dominates his discussions of those paradoxes we have remarked. In other contexts, however, Moore suggests a different and more complicated view—a view that is difficult to make out clearly. For example, he wrote in *Ethics:*

The truth is that there is an important distinction, which is not always observed, between what a man *means* by a given assertion and what he *expresses* by it. Whenever we make any assertion whatever (unless we do not mean what we say) we are always *expressing* one or other of two things—namely, either that we *think* the thing in question to be so or that we *know* it to be so. If, for instance, I say 'A is B', and mean what I say, what I mean is always merely that A *is* B; but those words of mine will always also express either the fact that I *think* that A is B, or the fact that I *know* it to be so; and even where I do not mean what I say, my words may be said to imply either that I think that A is B or that I know it, since they will commonly lead people to suppose that one or the other of these two things is the case.[12]

In drawing this distinction between meaning and expression Moore appears to say that, while meaning is more central, expression is also intimately connected with what is said. We

12. *Ethics* (London: Oxford University Press, 1949), p. 78.

always express belief when we assert things, Moore says, except when we don't mean what we say. Why does he make this exception? I believe Moore thought it was logically impossible to express a belief or an attitude one doesn't have, just as it is impossible to give away something one doesn't have. On the other hand, there is no such restriction on asserting; one asserts something whether he intends to or not, provided his words carry that meaning. Expression, like implying, is only a step-child of meaning. What is said is still central.

Later, in his notes, Moore explored the concept of expression further, giving a somewhat different account. He suggested that the sense in which we 'express' belief when we assert is the same as that 'in which a child's cries express his feelings or desires or emotions," even though these cries are not part of the language, are not names for anything. Because of the inference others can make from it about one's feelings, something is said to be an expression.[13] But this does not depend on one's intentions, and clearly not on one's actual feelings. The connection, Moore seems inclined to say, may be causal.

These remarks, though sketchy, show a radical departure in Moore's thought from the package theory. They suggest that the connection between one's beliefs and the words one utters enters very fundamentally into language. Moore is even led to the following observation, reminiscent of Wittgenstein:

The origin of language is, perhaps, not like the first use of language by the child, to name things which the person addressed can see as well as the person addressing; but to warn the person addressed of things he cannot see. As when a savage has discovered enemies approaching, & runs to warn the tribe of their approach; or has discovered a herd of deer, & runs to fetch the tribe to hunt; or has left his chief wounded, & runs to fetch help. Thus its prototype would be the warning bark of a dog. Nothing, can we say? would get a name, unless there were occasion to refer to

13. *Commonplace Book*, pp. 44–45.

it in its absence? or at least in its absence to the person addressed, in the sense of not being perceived by him.[14]

Here there is no mention of a conventional or customary connection. The connection between what is expressed and what is said is vital. It lies at the heart of what 'communication with language' is. In taking this direction, I will argue, Moore was on the right track to solving the paradoxes which so intrigued him.

I wish to call attention to one more issue raised by Moore which is connected with the others above. It arises in the province of ethics but it—like the paradox of saying that something is right but one doesn't approve of it—has its analogue in the province of belief. A consequence of the view Moore presented in *Ethics* is the paradox that a man ought to do what *he believes* is right even when it is not right; and conversely, that he ought not to do a thing which *he believes* to be wrong even though it is right. Moore wrote: "And we are thus committed to the paradox that a man may really deserve the strongest moral condemnation for choosing an action, which actually is right."[15] This paradox has the analogue in non-ethical assertions that a man ought to say what he believes, even though it should be false; and a man may be condemned for lying even when what he says is true. It will be my purpose to show that our beliefs are so intimately connected with our assertions that this 'paradox' is instead a thoroughly natural and suitable consequence.

2

We need to look more closely at that persuasive view of language learning which is associated with the package theory.[16] According to it, a child first learns various words,

14. *Ibid.*, p. 48.

15. *Ethics*, p. 121. Moore adds that this 'pardox' is nonetheless acceptable.

16. I have not identified the package theory with any particular philosopher, since it is very pervasive and was so at the time Moore

like color words and the names of objects, in learning 'games'
where he must sort and identify pictures or objects. The sorting is proposed by someone who knows the language and observes how the child proceeds, correcting wrong responses
and encouraging right ones. The child masters the sorting as
he might master some other skill, making fewer errors with
more repetitions, and he eventually comes to sort and identify
perfectly. When such a child has learned a vocabulary of
nouns, adjectives, adverbs in this way, he learns to use whole
sentences in a similar way. He correlates a sentence with a
certain situation: 'There goes the cat' belongs to one situation;
'The door stands open' belongs to another. The *use* of sentences is governed by rules which connect the sentences with
things going on in the world. Rules govern their use just as
rules in a game govern the moves there, much as the rules of
arithmetic and algebra govern the way in which a calculation
is done. When a child has learned the language, he has learned
a variety of things which can be done with it by virtue of its
rules and correlations, much as he might learn another skill
and how to use it.

It happens commonly that a child is taught to name all the
animals in a picture book by such a method as this. An adult
observes his performance, correcting errors and supplying
words that are forgotten. The situation is something like a
game, but like a game where at every point there is a *correct*
or *right move*. This corresponds to a drill, as do a spelling bee
and a multiplication quiz. And we surely do learn a great deal
this way, including fundamental calculations in arithmetic.
However, there is a great deal in our learning a language
which this account fails to explain.

---

wrote. It can be found in the thinking of Russell, Wittgenstein, and
many others. For a more detailed discussion of this and other views of
meaning I refer the reader to P. F. Strawson, *Logico Linguistic Papers*
(London: Methuen, 1971), especially the papers "Meaning and Truth"
and "Intention and Convention in Speech Acts."

Imagine, for example, that a child has learned to use color words and a number of nouns and that he can put these into simple sentences. So during one game he can answer the question, 'What is that?' with the sentence, 'That is a yellow sedan'; and he can answer the question, 'What do you see?' with the sentence 'I see a running zebra.' He can also answer a variety of questions about colors, using sentences like 'That is pale yellow,' 'This is lighter than that,' and 'Purple is darker than orange.' He has mastered a large vocabulary and a considerable amount of grammar.

I propose now that we imagine this child's mastery to be limited in a curious way. He never uses language *outside* the context of some game or drill. If he is set a problem in arithmetic, he does it; if he is asked a question to which there is a right answer, he answers it. If there is no right answer, he acts puzzled, remains silent. So when someone points to a yellow patch and asks what color it is, he answers. If someone asks him to count the apples in a basket he does it. But he never *volunteers* a remark, and he never asserts anything to someone *who does not already know the thing he asserts.*

What is missing in his use of language? Can we say that his skill is deficient? He answers all questions correctly. How can we identify a failure? If his training does train him for *language use,* then he should have mastered the latter in mastering the former. But something is fundamentally wrong with this notion of learning a language. What is missing is described by Rush Rhees:

If someone learns to speak, he does not just learn to make sentences and utter them. Nor can he merely have learned to react to orders. If that were all he ever did, I should not imagine that he could speak, and I should never ask him anything. When he learns to speak, he learns to tell you something; and he tries to.[17]

17. *Discussions of Wittgenstein* (London: Routledge and Kegan Paul, 1970), p. 79.

67993

What is missing in our example is the child's use of language to tell someone something. That was what his training was for. Rhees made the remark above in the course of a criticism of Wittgenstein's practice of comparing language to a calculus, and the learning of language to learning to calculate. The two kinds of learning are quite different, Rhees argues:

Wittgenstein used to speak of teaching a child to multiply by going through examples of multiplication for him, then getting him to go through these and through other exercises while you corrected his mistakes, and then saying, 'Go on by yourself now.' But if you said anything similar about teaching a child to speak you would have left out the most important thing. If he can speak, he has got something to tell you. In arithmetic it is different. Telling you things is not part of his achievement when he learns to multiply.[18]

In my example what is missing is the child's use of language to tell someone something. Without being asked, he never says to someone expecting a cab, 'A cab is waiting'; he never volunteers to someone going out, 'It's raining.' He never tells someone who doesn't already know it that he has a cold, or that he has been to a show. It is not exactly that he hasn't learned the language; rather he lacks the conception what language *is* and what it is *for*. And this is, as Rhees says, "the most important thing." It is moreover something which cannot be found by studying language learning in terms of training. Moore said that it belongs to the origins of language that words should be used when the person addressed couldn't observe what was referred to. It is not just the origins of language for which this holds; it is true of language in its primary function. Moore's remark points to the discrepancy between language training and language use. Looking at the former, we are led easily to the package theory or, with more sophistication, to the analogy between language and a calculus. But in taking this direc-

18. *Ibid.*, p. 80.

tion we are misled. We cannot account in this way for how language works.

The inability to use language in order to tell someone something appears very curious, somewhat like a psychological disorder. Why don't we observe this disability among children? Is it because language instruction is so thorough, so excellent? One must expect that something besides instruction is involved. Something in the child's experience tells him that speech is not typically a kind of game, not typically an activity of responding to someone else's move and responding in a way the other knows to be right or not. What a child observes of the people around him is that telling people things involves the speaker's initiative, his purposes, his beliefs, and his expectation of being trusted.

Suppose a child is taught various words in a variety of games and drills: how does he come to use those same sentences outside the games? What makes him think they can be used that way? The question is put wrong. Obviously the child observes adults using language before he practices the games. They do not sit down and sort cards or leaf through picture books when they use the sentence 'There's a dog.' They report what they see out of the window, and tell events witnessed during a walk, and say they remember where they left things. And in these typical uses, the person addressed does not already know whether the sentence is true. The child's training in language begins with these observations and his recognition of involvement in a language-using group. He too is told things, asked things, reminded of them. Formal games, then, are only a small part of his apprenticeship in language, as learning the shapes of various tools is only a small part of becoming a carpenter. The formal training alone doesn't show what language is; that is because *the training resembles a game*, while language use does not.

Both the package theory and Wittgenstein's calculus model misrepresent the learning of language and so the concept of language. And this misrepresentation lays the groundwork for paradoxes like Moore's. I will explain how it does.

The use of language to tell someone something involves the sincere expression of belief on one side and trust on the other. But precisely how are these involved? They are not necessary conditions, for then it would be impossible to lie and impossible to disbelieve what one is told. How then are they connected to the correct use of language?

The package theory postulates that a sentence is correlated with a situation which makes it true, and that learning a language consists in learning such correlations. Let us imagine this peculiar case: Imagine a person who generally tells us things he doesn't believe. He tells us there was frost in the night, and there was frost; yet he acts on the contrary belief. He tells us there is someone at the door, and someone is there; yet he shows by his behavior that he did not think so. What is wrong here? We cannot simply correct the sentences he uses, for they are true. What sentences could better fit those circumstances? The 'correlation' between sentence and situation is perfect. Then what protest can we make? Suppose we tell him he spoke misleadingly to us. Might he not reply that he certainly did not mislead us, nor did he intend to? Might he say that the truth of what he asserts is one thing, but what he believes is something different? What he believes, he argues, is his own affair. It does not enter what he says. How on earth should we answer this?

We want to insist that his beliefs are involved in his assertions. What he seems to have misunderstood is the nature of asserting—what kind of thing it is. For if he understood this, he would not imagine he could assert things without expressing his belief, truly or falsely. Indeed, expression of belief seems more fundamental to asserting than the truth or falsity of what is asserted. For consider that it is no defense of an insincere assertion that it is true, while it is a defense of a false assertion that it was what one believed. The situation here is analogous to the one Moore remarked in ethics: we censure a person for speaking falsely, that is, insincerely, as we censure a person who does what he thinks is wrong. In both cases what is true (right) appears secondary to whether a person speaks (acts) according to what he believes to be true (right).

Why can't a person use the sentence 'There was frost in the night' in a *neutral* way? Why cannot he mean only something about the frost and nothing about himself? After all, may not his thoughts, being private, be privately held?[19] The answer is that his assertions do express beliefs. This is a characteristic of their normal use. Having a particular intention is not a necessary condition for the expression of belief. Nothing besides the assertion is needed. Similarly, a particular intention to mislead need not be added to saying something without a belief that it is so. To say what one doesn't believe is to speak misleadingly. Moore was right that addition of a certain intention is not necessary for asserting; simply to assert *is* to express a belief.

We are led by such considerations as these toward a conception of the meaning of sentences like 'The cat has been fed,' 'I went to the pictures,' which incorporates the expression of belief into the notion of using a sentence to tell someone something. We are led, that is, to a certain alternative to the package theory. According to it, sentences which are used to tell someone something simply do express the speaker's beliefs. They express beliefs without the addition of any intention. They do this because it is their role to do it within the framework of the language. In this role they can be used to mislead, but in normal contexts they cannot be used neutrally.

This is not to say that telling someone something is the only

19. This manner of reasoning exhibits our tendency to separate 'inner' thoughts and feelings from 'outer' behavior, including speech. A correct view of the nature of language, as I see it, does not allow such a separation.

use of such sentences. Consider the following use, which is quite different: A person is charged with relaying messages and to repeat exactly what he hears. He is therefore expected to utter sentences—for example, 'There was frost in the night'—whether he believes them or not. In this job his utterances do not express his beliefs. He could not be said to speak falsely, that is, insincerely, when he says something without believing it. Perhaps we would not even say he *asserts* the things he says; perhaps we would not say he is *telling* anyone that there was frost.[20] But most certainly we would not say he was lying, just as we wouldn't say he was sincere either. His use of these sentences must be understood in terms of the job he is charged to do, and not as the most normal or usual use. That this is so can be seen by noticing that, should he utter the same sentences after his work day is over, he should then be taken to be expressing his beliefs. He doesn't need to add a particular signal. That he is speaking now like the rest of us is enough.

It would be an error to deny that there are other nonbelief-expressing uses of such sentences. The sentences may occur in a poem, to evoke some feeling; they may be used in a coded message, saying something different from what they normally do; they may occur as titles, lines in a song, watchwords, metaphors, and the like. But their most usual and typical and important use is to tell something to someone, and in this use they express beliefs.

The concept of belief-expression helps illuminate the relation of 'lying' to that of 'correct use.' It is baffling how we should distinguish lying from misusing a sentence that is believed false. The two concepts seem to coincide, both standing in contrast to 'correct use.' The truth is that sentences like 'The cat has been fed' ordinarily express belief. And this fea-

20. Max Black, in an examination of Moore's paradox, suggests that the key to the absurdity is that Moore's sentence cannot be used to *assert* anything ("Saying and Disbelieving," *Analysis*, 13 (Dec. 1952), 28–31). I agree, but this by itself doesn't explain what is paradoxical.

ture allows us to lie, that is, misrepresent our beliefs. It would be a misuse, on the other hand, to use the sentence as if it expressed *no belief at all*, for this would show a misunderstanding about its role.

I return again to Moore's explanation of why truth-telling is important to the absurdity of his sentence. He says that we all "learn by experience that in the immense majority of cases a man who makes such an assertion [as that he went to the pictures last Tuesday] . . . does believe or know what he asserts: lying, though common enough, is vastly exceptional."[21] We saw that this does not account for the absurdity of 'I went to the pictures, but I don't believe that I did.' What does account for it is that the expression of belief belongs to the sentence as part of its meaning. It is not adaptation to custom that accounts for our telling the truth but our understanding of human utterance as a practice. The absurd sentence is self-vitiating. One cannot make anything of it—not a lie or a misrepresentation or anything else comprehensible. It is incoherent. (Whether it is also contradictory will be discussed in Section 4, below.)

It has become a commonplace in philosophy that truth-telling is a factually necessary condition for language. If the majority of people lied, speech would be useless. What I propose is a stronger claim: Understanding the need for truth-telling follows directly from understanding language as a means of telling someone something. This function of language makes lying possible and makes it feasible. The connection is not contingent but conceptual.

I turn now to develop the notion of belief-expression more fully and to relate it specifically to the issues raised by Moore's paradox.

3

If we are asked to consider 'the meaning of the sentence "I went to the pictures last Tuesday," ' what is it we are to

21. "A Reply to My Critics," pp. 542–543.

consider? Do we direct our attention to its use as a line of poetry? Should we think of a parrot uttering these words? Should we think of it as a story title? Obviously we wouldn't think of any of these uses. We would think of its use to express a belief, to tell something to someone, in some everyday situation. Imagine, on the contrary, that we were *not* to think of this use. Imagine we were to think only of its nonbelief-expressing uses. How can we do that? The other uses seem derivative from the belief-expressing one. For example, we understand the title of a story when we finish the story, when we see how that expression connects with the events and persons mentioned. To consider the meaning of a title by itself is practically impossible. And the same can be said for the parrot's utterance, for metaphorical and evocative uses. When a philosopher asks us to consider the meaning of this sentence, he surely wants us to think of its use to tell someone something. The fundamental—the central—meaning of this sentence is concerned with the expression of belief.

The expression of a belief is essential to the meaning of the sentences in Moore's paradox. If one of these sentences is used so as not to express a belief on some occasion, that use is not its most normal or typical one. The meaning of the sentence is normally connected with trust and the expression of belief. I will argue that these characteristics, which allow the sentence to be useful for giving information, also cannot be separated from discussions of its 'truth.'

First consider whether there is any way of distinguishing sentences that are belief-expressing from other kinds. Is there some criterion by which these sentences can be identified? Although I do not know of a sufficient condition, there is a necessary one, a *sine qua non* of belief-expressing sentences. It is this: We can always ask of a belief-expressing utterance whether it is sincere or not; therefore a sentence which is normally belief-expressing will also be one which is normally used so that sincerity and insincerity meaningfully apply to it.

Someone who asserts that he went to the pictures last Tuesday is either sincere or insincere in his assertion. And so is someone who asserts that there was frost or that a taxi is waiting or any of the countless things we tell to others. Other kinds of sentences are characterized by this mark, however—expressions of pain, anxiety, self-confidence, indignation, and the like. Such sentences as 'Oh dear!,' 'It hurts,' 'How could you!' are also characteristically either sincere or not. Therefore this mark does not serve positively to identify belief-expressing sentences, but only helps us identify nonbelief-expressing ones.

We can easily see that some sentences are not normally used to express beliefs. For instance, sentences of arithmetic, logic, and geometry are not. Consider how they are learned: they are learned in the process of learning kinds of calculation and proof. They are mastered as part of a skill. If someone utters the sentence '5 + 4 = 9' in the course of calculating, it is part of what he is doing, just as it is when a person mutters directions to himself when following a complicated procedure. Someone overhearing such a speaker would not ask whether the remark is sincere, nor would he assume he was being addressed. But cannot a teacher use the sentence sincerely when teaching arithmetic? He says to the class, "5 + 4 = 9"; is he expressing his belief in the sense he does when he says that lunch hour is almost over? One cannot find the cases alike. The numerical sentence is part of a drill, of training. And the aim of the training is proficient calculation; its aim is not the communication of beliefs. The student who mutters it to himself while calculating is not using it that way either. Calculating and telling someone something, as Rhees observed, are utterly different activities. So we should expect that the sentences used in them have different kinds of meaning.

A similar argument can be made for sentences occurring in mathematical or geometrical proofs. Imagine questioning the sincerity of someone who is presenting a proof. Even if the presentation is a sophisticated joke, this is not analogous to telling a lie. A formal proof does not involve the expression of beliefs. To see this it helps to try to imagine taking a proof on trust, taking it on the authority of the person giving it as one takes a statement on authority in matters of geology or history. Accepting a proof this way vitiates its force *as a proof!* It cannot function as a sincere expression of belief and remain a proof.

Rhees' assertion that sentences of arithmetic are more like moves in a game than other kinds of sentences are is right. It is possible to give a proof in order to deceive someone, but the deception is not the same as lying. And so a storekeeper may use a false arithmetical sentence in the course of cheating a customer, or do a calculation wrong, but these would not be cases of lying. The reason is, belief was not in the first instance expressed by these things.

If there is a sharp line between such nonbelief-expressing sentences and sentences that normally express beliefs, is it possible to describe and identify the latter as a class? Is it possible to describe a class of sentences to which Moore's paradox might apply, for example, the class of 'factual' or 'empirical' sentences? If so, we must be able to draw the line between sentences that are normally 'factual' and those that are normally fictional. Is a belief expressed by 'There are three unicorns'? In a story about unicorns that sentence might express the belief of some character. But what does this evidence amount to when the only normal use of such a sentence is in a story? Or again: how should we view the normal use of sentences about inhabitants of the planet Jupiter? Their normal use now may be in story-telling, but they may become belief-expressing—just as sentences about travel to the moon, once principally fictional in use, came to express beliefs. To identify which sentences do and which do not express belief one has to examine and take note of what is believed. Looking at a sentence will not decide it.

There are other sentences whose role depends on a consideration of actual use. Those containing figurative expressions are one kind. What belief is expressed by saying a person has many irons in the fire? Not a belief about irons or fires. The expression of belief and the character of the belief can be determined only by seeing what the use is. Another kind of sentence that presents difficulty is the class of sentences we learn by rote as part of our education, for example, the atomic weights of elements. These things were learned perhaps in the same way by our teachers. When sentences about them are asserted, do they express beliefs? To determine this, one has to consider whether their use may be sincere or not, and the answer will be for one person "Yes" and for another "No." The use of such sentences and whether they express beliefs must therefore be referred to a certain context and a certain kind of speaker. For some people their use may resemble the use of number sentences by an accountant; for others their use may resemble a firsthand laboratory finding.

We cannot tell just by looking at them whether sentences serve to express belief or not. Perhaps then it is misleading to speak of a class of such sentences. For we then have to deal with the difference made by any eccentric whose use of a sentence differs from ours. It is more reasonable to say that there is no definite class of sentences expressing beliefs.

The claim that we need to refer to a context to understand a sentence's meaning conflicts with the package theory, because it goes against the assumption that a meaning is recognizable from a sentence alone. One has a powerful inclination, however, to make this protest: After all, a sentence can have a clear meaning and even be true although no one has ever believed or uttered it. There are empirical truths not yet discovered; are they not meaningful now? And sentences may be true even though people use them to chase demons or think them false or ridiculous. The meaning and truth of a sentence are independent of what we believe and independent of what we say.[22] Therefore the account of meaning which involves contexts and belief expression must be wrong.

This objection raises a large question much discussed in recent philosophy. It seems very natural to say that a sentence or proposition can be true even though it is never thought or formulated—that truth is something apart from the practices or beliefs of any society. On my view, however, this issue exemplifies the confusion introduced by supposing that propositions are the objects of our belief. It follows from my account that the issue whether a belief-expressing sentence is true arises only upon treating it as an expression of belief. To ask whether something is true is to raise the question whether such a belief would be true. There is no abstract issue of truth apart from this. This is not to say that someone must hold a particular belief in order for its truth to come into question. It is only to say that the sentence must be treated *as a belief-expressing one*, and its truth dealt with as the truth of someone's belief.

The general claim that truth and belief are thus closely bound together was once expressed by P. F. Strawson:

> When we come to try to explain in general what it is to say something true, to express a true proposition, reference to belief or to assertion (and thereby to belief) is inescapable. Thus we may harmlessly venture: Someone says something true if things are as he says they are. But this 'says' already has the force of 'asserts' . . .
>
> Reference, direct or indirect, to belief expression is inseparable from the analysis of saying something true (or false.)[23]

Strawson believes that we are misled here by our inclination to speak of truth in the abstract, to speak of 'true' as a predicate of 'type-sentences'—sentences taken in themselves and apart from a context or use. He warns against this practice:

22. This subject is discussed more fully in Chapter V, Section 2; also in Chapter VI, Section 1.
23. *Logico Linguistic Papers*, p. 189.

For if we are not careful . . . it is liable, when we inquire into the nature of meaning, to make us forget what sentences are *for*. We connect meaning with truth and truth, too simply, with sentences; and sentences belong to language. But, as theorists, we know nothing of human *language* unless we understand human *speech*.[24]

His point here is similar to Rhees'; if we look to the use of language to tell someone something we find this use essentially connected with beliefs. The final explanation of meaning, Strawson believes, would involve references to the community of individuals whose purposes the language serves.[25]

Strawson holds that the tendency to speak of the truth of type-sentences is a careless habit. We need to guard against its implications, for they mislead us. Yet where does this tendency come from? The answer is not hard to find. When we speak of a truth of arithmetic, it is the sentence which interests us and receives attention. We are not then concerned with anyone's belief or the expression of it: such sentences don't express beliefs. Therefore their truth is independent of belief. If one utterance of such a sentence is true, all are. Truth here is really a predicate of the type-sentence.

Behind the notion that truth is a predicate of type-sentences is our inclination to use mathematical sentences as the model for other kinds. I have shown, however, that the meaning of these is distinctive, for they do not express beliefs. Sincerity and insincerity are irrelevant to them. It is not surprising then that their truth is distinctive as well.[26] Taking arithmetical sentences as the model for belief-expressing ones means that our account of the latter will be wrong. My view on this differs

24. *Ibid.*
25. *Ibid.*, pp. 187–188.
26. Wittgenstein, discussing the truth of sentences of logic, added the qualification "in, e.g., Russell's system" (*Remarks on the Foundations of Mathematics* [Oxford: Blackwell, 1956], App. I, 6–7), thus explicitly relating the truth of these sentences to a formal system.

from Strawson's, for he thinks one account of meaning will be satisfactory to both.

Consider for a moment what it means to say an arithmetical sentence is *true*. If a child acts uncertain while reciting multiplication sentences, we might reassure him, saying, "That's true," or "That's right," or "That's the way." We are encouraging him in his recitation. But is there any other use of the sentence 'That's true' applicable to number sentences? Would we say it to an adult who asserts it? But when would he do that?[27] We are at a loss to say, for we cannot imagine it being used to express a belief. We feel compelled to say that it *is true*, but we cannot show what point there would be in saying this. It is a dead end.

Truth is generally not a type-sentence predicate when it concerns an expression of belief. It is not hard to see why this is so. We do not determine the truth of the sentence 'The cat has been fed' by examining the sentence or constructing a proof. These things are irrelevant. Nor would it serve any purpose to determine its truth this way, once and for all.[28] 'The cat has been fed' has a new function each day; it answers a question which may arise each day; there is no 'truth' which applies to it over a longer time. That is a feature of its use. Philosophers have sometimes thought there is no harm in making the meaning more specific, so that when we speak of its truth we are speaking of one occasion only. The introduction of designations of time and location and identity serve to

27. Norman Malcolm once described circumstances for saying this, but they are very curious ones, and Malcolm admits it is an unusual thing to say (*Knowledge and Certainty*, p. 63). For a discussion of Malcolm's example, see Chapter VII, Section 1.

28. Proofs of propositions in physics and the like may provide exceptions to this generalization. Propositions of physics are not like propositions of arithmetic, logic, or geometry. But do they express beliefs? Perhaps they have a mixed character, mixed uses. More needs to be considered about their actual use to determine whether their 'truth' is that of type-sentences or not.

do this, so that instead of 'The cat has been fed' we have 'Jeremiah the cat has been fed at our house on April 24th 1975 at 6:00 P.M.' Now this sentence has truth as a type-sentence predicate. But it is plainly a grotesque substitute for the original. That was a sentence with multiple uses, one whose truth on each occasion may be a new question. It is essentially re-cyclable, reusable, and this depends upon it *not* having truth as a type-sentence predicate.[29]

The differences I emphasize here entail that there cannot be one account of meaning or one account of truth for mathematical and nonmathematical sentences alike. To give such an account, one must have sentences cut to fit it. And then what about our everyday sentences? Have they no meaning worth accounting for? And what makes us think that mathematical truth should be taken as the model for truth in general? One might argue even that necessary truth, being so distinctive and specialized, is not really truth at all; for it is truth of another kind that we most commonly refer to and consider.

4

I turn to Moore's explanation of why the sentence 'I went to the pictures last Tuesday but I don't believe I did' is para-doxical. It is paradoxical because it says something that is con-tradicted by what is implied by saying it. The sentence is not a contradiction, because it doesn't say two contradictory

29. Imagine how curious it would be if sentences could normally only be used once. One could not ask if 'The cat is gone' or 'Spinach is today's soup' or 'The road is icy' are true again today, or whether they may be true tomorrow as they were yesterday. This curious consequence comes from the philosophically unsettling fact that the world of change and becoming does not hold still for us to know it. Plato would say that for real knowledge we need eternal objects—objects whose truth and meaning are both fixed. Having these, we can regard the world of change and changing truths as mere appearance. This is a more colorful way of saying that truth is essentially a type-sentence predicate.

things nor are two contradictory things implied by what it says. So Moore infers that the belief that the speaker didn't go to the pictures is involved in the meaning only *by implication* in his special sense of 'implies.' There would be a contradiction only if the belief were more directly expressed. There is a mistake in this reasoning.

I have argued that the expression of belief is directly involved in the meaning of such sentences. Therefore it is not a more direct expression of one's belief to say 'I *believe* I went to the pictures' than to say 'I went to the pictures.' But if this is so, why does the term 'contradiction' only apply if the sentence goes: 'I believe I went to the pictures and I don't believe that I did'? The answer commonly given is that this has the *form* of a contradiction which the other lacks. But putting forms aside, one must wonder what is the function of 'I believe' added to a flat assertion. If the flat assertion already expresses belief, what is added by this phrase?

Saying that the cat has been fed is different from saying one thinks the cat has been fed. Yet if the former expresses belief, shouldn't these be equivalent? What is the difference? If you compare the sentences, you observe that one is weaker than the other. The flat statement is stronger; saying one believes or thinks the cat has been fed is weaker than saying it has been fed. If someone says he believes the troops are advancing, he is being more tentative than if he said flatly that they are advancing. Furthermore, the more he emphasizes the word 'believe,' the more his qualification is being emphasized. In saying he believes, he is expressing less conviction than if he said nothing about belief at all.

Is this not paradoxical? Is it not paradoxical that the phrase 'I believe' is less an expression of firm belief than simply asserting whatever it attaches to? It is paradoxical if one assumes that we can see on the face of an expression how it functions. We are puzzled here if we assume that expressions of belief generally or always involve the use of such a phrase as 'I believe.' But I have argued that the practice of expressing beliefs is much wider than the use of 'I believe,' and the function of that phrase is in consequence a specialized one. Its function is to signal the expression of a weak belief; stronger forms of belief expression have no signal.

A careful description of the use of 'I believe' helps us to understand some otherwise puzzling observations about belief—for example, that it is a 'weak attitude' as contrasted with that of certainty or conviction. Yet are these latter not also forms of belief? Then why should 'I believe' be weaker than they? It did not seem paradoxical to Prichard, for instance, that "on the one hand we should only say that we know something when we are certain of it, and conversely; . . . whereas, on the other hand, when we believe something we are uncertain of it."[30] When we believe a thing, we are uncertain of it— that can't be right! Yet Prichard draws this conclusion from supposing that the use of 'believe' represents the expression of belief. H. H. Price in explaining the 'performatory' character of saying one believes a thing—by analogy to saying one knows—shows himself to be drawn in opposite directions. He says that most commonly, in saying 'I believe that p' "We are inviting our hearers to accept what we believe and are assuming that they will. And we are doing more than that. We are conveying to them, giving them to understand, that they will be *justified* in accepting it."[31] Yet while we give an assurance of sorts in this way, it is much weaker than what we give by saying we know.

'Is Wilkinson in Oxford to-day?' 'Yes, I believe he is.' In giving this answer, one conveys to one's hearer that he may safely rely to a certain degree upon the truth of the proposition 'Wilkinson is in Oxford to-day', but not that he may safely rely on it without any reservations at all. . . . Indeed, it might seem too much to

30. H. A. Prichard, *op. cit.*, p. 88.
31. *Belief* (London: Allen and Unwin, 1969), p. 30.

say that this utterance gives us anything which deserves to be called a guarantee. All the same, it does give us something.[32]

What a confusing picture this gives! What 'I believe' seems to express—one's conviction—it is seen not to express when contrasted with 'I know.' Price appears to be misled by thinking that what the phrase *says* is what it *means*. But what it says is belied by its most common uses, and in particular by its uses in contrast to the use of 'I know' or with a flat unqualified assertion. To say that it expresses a guarantee, but only a weak one, is to hedge on what would otherwise appear as a contradiction. And his conclusion that 'I believe' "does give us something" is the admission of his evident confusion.

The paradox of Prichard's remark and the contradiction of Price's conclusion both arise from the assumption that the use of 'I believe' reveals how we express beliefs. Yet neither philosopher investigated whether this is so. They would otherwise have found that it expresses hesitation while firmer expressions of belief contain no reference to belief. Expressions of belief are often just flat assertions.

Another curiosity of theories of knowledge can also be explained by such an account of 'I believe.' It has often seemed that believing and knowing are exclusive, exclusive states perhaps, because one generally would not say he *believes* a thing which he says he *knows*.[33] He says one or the other, according to the firmness of his belief. It is plausible then to suppose he represents one or the other of two states in so choosing. Yet it is obvious on the other hand that if he knows a thing he must believe it! And now we seem to have a contradiction: are knowing and believing exclusive, or does one entail the other? The solution lies in noticing that the first person uses of 'I be-

32. *Ibid.*, p. 31.
33. Prichard clearly held this, as did Price in his paper "Some Considerations About Belief" (included in A. P. Griffiths, ed., *Knowledge and Belief* [London: Oxford University Press, 1967], pp. 41ff).

lieve' are not analogous to the third person uses. 'I believe' is contrasted with 'I know,' and each excludes the other on a given occasion. But 'He knows' is not contrasted with 'He believes'; on the contrary, his knowing entails his believing. The contradiction dissolves when we see that the first person uses of 'believe' and 'know' are expressive in ways that the third person uses are (by necessity) not.

Moore suggests that what is implied by a person's utterance is, in not being part of the meaning, being conveyed indirectly; and he accounts for this by reference to customs or conventions. On his view of meaning it would be a more direct expression of belief to say *that one believes* rather than assert what one believes. My account shows that, on the contrary, the expression of belief is most commonly given by asserting what one believes. My account has the consequence, then, that what is expressed by us in our expressions of belief may not be translatable into something which is said. That is, we cannot reduce what is expressed (e.g. our belief) to some phrase which says the same thing (i.e. that we believe). For the making of any such translation alters the meaning. In this my account conflicts with a common philosophical assumption—that meaning involves principally what is said or asserted, and that whatever one expresses or implies might have been asserted instead. Such a view is stated by John Searle in his 'Principle of Expressibility," the principle that what is expressed could just as well be said.[34] Such a thesis guarantees that whatever is expressed, and therefore whatever is sincere or insincere in one's assertions, could have been said, and so been simply true or false. The principle guarantees the reducibility of the expressive dimension of our language to that of saying. It is my view that there is no more direct, primary, or explicit way of expressing one's beliefs than simply asserting what one believes. This *is* the primary form, and it derives from the most rudimentary function of language. It derives

34. *Speech Acts*, pp. 19–21.

from using language to tell something to someone. The assumption that it can be 'reduced' or disposed of can only distort our idea of how language works.

Is Moore's paradoxical sentence contradictory? We cannot turn it into a formal contradiction by translation, and that might settle the question. For a contradiction by common accounts is either a sentence whose form is '*p and ∼p*' or a sentence from which a sentence of that form can be derived. And I argue that Moore's sentence cannot be put into a form where the conflict becomes explicit without its suffering some change of meaning. But I will argue that the paradoxical sentence is in a fundamental respect very like a contradiction and therefore can be thought of in the same way.

If Moore's sentence were 'I went to the pictures but I didn't go' it would be a contradiction. Is that a matter of its form alone? Is any sentence of the form '*p and ∼p*' a contradiction? We find uses for many sentences with this form or from which such a form is easily derivable: 'He is old but still young,' 'He is absent yet still with us,' 'They are dead yet they live on.' We don't call these contradictions. Why not? Perhaps it is because they have a use and so we understand them. 'They live on' does not contradict 'They died' *in this case* because we understand what is meant. The belief expressed by saying 'They died' does not conflict with the belief expressed by 'They live on.' The form of words or the derivation of a contradictory form of words does not guarantee the presence of a genuine contradiction. Then what does? The presence of a conflict in beliefs. What makes a contradiction what it is, is that one cannot *hold* it, one cannot believe both of the things it expresses. And this is why no one can sincerely assert a contradiction, although he can of course say the words.

This conflict is precisely what characterizes Moore's paradoxical sentence: one cannot assert it because one cannot believe both the things it expresses. For on the one hand it expresses the conviction that the speaker went to the pictures and on the other it expresses disbelief about the same matter. We have just the features necessary to make a sentence contradictory; all that is lacking is the form 'p and $\sim p$.'

How, then, can we explain the fact (which is stressed by Moore) that the sentence might all the same be true? Surely something that might be true is no contradiction! Our discussion of truth, however, showed that truth is related to belief—to suppositions, hypotheses, beliefs. And the issue of the 'truth' of Moore's sentence cannot arise, because that sentence cannot express a belief. It is self-vitiating.

The next question is whether Moore's sentence then lacks meaning. It is ostensibly a belief-expressing sentence, yet so constructed that it cannot express a belief. Is it then meaningless? I defer discussion of that until Chapter VI. For the present it is sufficient to remark that Moore's absurd proposition is a monster made of familiar parts, a creature formed by grammatical union. Such monsters are not uncommon, one might add, in the regions of philosophy.

5

Moore's paradox raises a number of fundamental questions for a philosophy of knowledge and belief. It raises, first, the question: What is involved in asserting a proposition—what is the relation between what a proposition says and what a speaker communicates by uttering it? This question bothered Moore in various connections, not least in connection with the Epimenides and liar paradoxes. In denying that a sentence can say of itself that it is false, he once said that every sentence says of itself that it is true—a really curious idea![35] Yet when one sees how intimately belief-expression and meaning and truth are connected in the case of belief-expressing sentences, the remark becomes a reflection (albeit distorted) of their

35. *Commonplace Book*, p. 313.

connection. A person who says that the cat has been fed is normally expressing his belief; part of the meaning of what he says is *that this is his belief*, though he does not say it is.

Second, the paradox raises the question: What is the relation of lying to correct use? To answer this we found it necessary to see sincerity and trust as parts of the concept of making an assertion, of telling something to someone. They are not, as is sometimes thought, contingently necessary conditions, but characterize language in this kind of communication. Nor are they unlike the sincerity and trust that are required for moral responsibility. A person's actions express his beliefs about what is right, and for someone to act against his beliefs is a violation of fundamental kind, a violation of the concept of morality as expressible and expressed in one's actions.

Third, Moore's paradox raises questions about the notion of 'contradictoriness,' and how central a particular form—'p and $\sim p$'—is to this notion. The concepts of contradiction and consistency play large roles in philosophical reasoning, yet these roles are by no means as simple as we often think. Indeed, it will be considered later whether these traditional concepts should be trusted at all—a question Moore himself comes near to raising.[36] For our understanding of Moore's paradox it is sufficient to see that his absurd sentence is very *like* a contradiction in possessing the chief property that characterizes these: it expresses conflicting beliefs.

Moore's paradox raises also the question how 'Moore went to the pictures but doesn't believe it' is related to 'I went to the pictures but don't believe it,' said by Moore. It forces us to look at the relation between first- and third-person sentences involving belief. In doing this we discover a striking disanalogy: we find that the phrase 'I believe' does not predicate

36. Further discussion of contradictions and Moore's remarks about some of them are found in Chapter VI, Section 3.

belief of me as 'he believes' does of someone else. On the contrary it expresses hesitancy and qualification, while 'he believes' neither expresses nor attributes such to him. This example warns us again not to take language as self-descriptive, as saying literally how its concepts work. 'I believe' does not mean that I believe as it seems to. Indeed, the more emphasis one puts on this phrase, the greater may be the qualification—the greater the hesitancy—one expresses.

Of the chief underlying sources of difficulty in Moore's discussion are these: first, the notion that propositions are the objects of belief; second, that they carry their meanings on their faces, that they *say* what they mean—this is the idea that what is meant is what is said, and that what is said is fundamental to what is implied or expressed. Third, the 'package theory' of meaning obscures the notion which is central if the paradox is to be solved—the notion of expressing belief. This notion is fundamental to our employment of language to tell something to someone.

V

The Belief that I Exist

Consequences flow from making the distinction between sentences expressing beliefs and other kinds of sentences. In this chapter and the next that distinction will be brought to bear on two perennially interesting matters: here on the proof that we exist, and in the next chapter on the 'common sense propositions' of G. E. Moore.

Descartes reasoned as follows: When we study to find the very beginning of our knowledge, the first and most basic and most unquestionable thing we know, nothing offers itself so immediately as the fact of our existence. For even as we ponder what we know, we must exist. If anything is certain beyond doubt this must be, for thinking itself confirms it. And if this is not known, how can anything else be? Our existence, then appears certain and provable beyond the possibility of doubt.[1]

1. Among the recent efforts to clarify the *cogito*, the following are of particular interest, and some will be referred to in the text: A. J. Ayer, " 'I Think, Therefore I Am,' " in W. Doney, ed., *Descartes* (Garden City, N.Y.: Anchor Books, 1967); J. Hintikka, "*Cogito, Ergo*

We give easy assent to this argument of the Second Meditation—Descartes's argument that he exists and knows he exists
because he thinks. Philosophers who count nothing else right
in Descartes's procedure agree to this step; and as it is compatible with even a radical doubt, this seems one point all
theories about knowledge might have in common.

Just the same one wonders that the proposition 'I exist,'
which is thought so fundamental, should also be considered
provable. How should such a proof arise? Perhaps, as in the
proofs of geometry which Descartes took as his models, he
should posit an unproved and self-evident beginning, as an
axiom or postulate. But such a beginning would not be fitting
in a proof of his existence. For that is a natural and contingent
fact and must be shown as facts are shown, not by way of
positing or defining. There seems a paradox in the very beginning of Descartes's program: on the one hand he seeks a
primitive certainty, a fixed point from which to proceed; on
the other he wishes to prove that this point is secure. How can
this seeming paradox be resolved? We must look at the way
Descartes conceives his proof to function, and the kinds of
formulations he gives. And we must examine too the proposition 'I exist,' which is to be proved, considering its claim to be
of central importance to the theory of knowledge. I will argue
that Descartes's treatment of this proposition reflects a mistaken view about its connection with beliefs. In particular I
argue that it is a mistake to hold that we have an everyday and
continuing belief in our existence.

1

In the First Meditation, Descartes proposes to sweep aside
all his former beliefs. He will do this by attacking "those prin-

Sum: Inference or Performance?" (also in W. Doney, ed.); A. Kenny,
Descartes (New York: Random House, 1968), Ch. 3; H. Frankfurt,
Demons, Dreamers and Madmen (New York: Bobbs-Merrill, 1970),
Ch. 1.

ciples upon which all my former beliefs rested."[2] He will reserve judgment about each of them until he can offer compelling proof that it is true. Descartes finds the effort required for this very great. He cannot easily shake off all those beliefs—"they occupy my mind against my inclinations." To guard against accepting them unawares, he conceives a stratagem: he will take "of set purpose a contrary belief . . . and for a certain time pretend that all these opinions are entirely false and imaginary."[3] He will assume that all his beliefs are false unless he can prove that one of them is not.

Descartes's procedure here is to adopt a hypothesis—that all his beliefs are false. Then he will test to see whether it is consistent, and being consistent, possibly true.[4] He will consider its consequences: does anything forbid them? Do they lead to contradiction? He must spell out what they are, as he does in this vivid passage: "I shall consider that the heavens, the earth, colours, figure, sound and all external things are nought but . . . illusions and dreams . . . ; I shall consider myself as having no hands, no eyes, no flesh, no blood, nor any senses."[5] The consequences, however bizarre, do not lead to contradiction. So far the hypothesis holds.

This procedure is not original with Descartes. It resembles classic procedures in geometry, where a hypothesis is given and

2. E. Haldane and G. R. T. Ross, trans., *The Philosophical Works of Descartes* (Cambridge: Cambridge University Press, 1967), I, 145 (hereafter in this chapter referred to as 'H.R.').

3. H.R., I, 148.

4. Descartes makes clear that he is not really doubting, in a letter to Bourdin, where he writes: "When I said that doubtful matters should sometimes be treated as though they were false, I clearly explained that I merely meant that, for the purpose of investigating truths that are metaphysically certain, we should pay no more attention to doubtful matters than to what is plainly false" (H.R., II, 266). The 'doubt' is really a hypothesis, a move to discover *whether* it is possible to doubt everything.

5. H.R., I, 148.

then shown to be false by a reduction to absurdity. Could two parallel lines meet? Let us suppose there are two which do; what follows from this? We encounter a contradiction. Then we have proved the hypothesis false and its negation true. Galileo used similar proofs in his work on mechanics.[6] Imagine a principle to hold, he would ask. Then imagine the consequences of it, delineating them in imagination and following their consequences in turn. Do we find any conflict with what is already known? If a conflict is found, we have a proof that the hypothesis is false. This kind of argument depends heavily on the author spelling out the consequences of his hypothesis, sometimes in great detail, for otherwise a telling inconsistency may be overlooked. The vivid description Descartes gives of what he is supposing is part of such an argument. It is not a spontaneous expression of doubt.

The First Meditation ends and the Second begins with this supposition that all Descartes's beliefs are false. Where does it lead? "What, then, can be esteemed as true? Perhaps nothing at all, unless that there is nothing in the world that is certain."[7] Perhaps only that the hypothesis states a real possibility. But while he is pondering, Descartes observes that anyway he must exist—"am I not at least something?"[8] Of course! How else could he make the hypothesis? That he exists is certain even though possibly nothing else is.

Without entering the moment of Descartes's pondering and

6. Such an example can be found in the First Day of *The Two New Sciences* where Simplicio complains: "The argument and demonstrations which you have advanced are mathematical, abstract, and far removed from concrete matter; and I do not believe that when applied to the physical and natural world these laws will hold" (H. Crew and A. de Salvio, trans. [New York: Dover, 1914], p. 52). Salviati responds by describing a physical situation in detail and tracing the consequences. An appeal to the imagination is substituted for a formal proof. It is an instance of a *Gedankenexperiment*.

7. H.R., I, 149.

8. *Ibid.*, p. 150.

his discovery, can we state the form of this argument? Can we show its compelling character as an argument? That is not easy, partly because Descartes leads us in conflicting ways. From the outset we took his intention to be the testing of the hypothesis 'All my beliefs are false.' If this were his purpose, his conclusion should be either 'All my beliefs may be false,' or 'Not all my beliefs may be false.' But neither of these is his conclusion. Instead he seems to conclude that he exists. How is this possible? The argument is now obscure.

But it is also unclear just what Descartes means to conclude. For in the same Meditation he states as his conclusion, not that he exists, but that "I am, I exist, is necessarily true each time that I pronounce it or that I mentally conceive it."[9] And a reader soon realizes that the shift is not just careless. If one turns to the *Discourse* for help, one finds the same difficulty there. Descartes writes about making his hypothesis, and then tells us:

But immediately afterwards I noticed that whilst I thus wished to think all things false, it was absolutely essential that the 'I' who thought this should be somewhat, and remarking that this truth '*I think, therefore I am*' was so certain and so assured that all the most extravagant suppositions brought forward by the sceptics were incapable of shaking it, I came to the conclusion that I could receive it without scruple as the first principle of Philosophy for which I was seeking.[10]

He seems to say here that his conclusion is 'I must be somewhat' and also that it is 'I think, therefore I am.' But it clearly cannot be both. Then which does he refer to when he speaks of 'it' being the first principle of philosophy?[11]

9. *Ibid.*

10. *Ibid.*, p. 101; Descartes's italics.

11. These vacillations have long puzzled philosophers and are considered in nearly every major work on the Second Meditation, including those of Frankfurt and Kenny (above, n. 1). My own explanation of them is given in the Appendix to this chapter.

I propose we begin by comparing some of the various forms Descartes's argument takes—or is described as taking—and take note of their virtues both as arguments and as fulfilling Descartes's purpose, supposing that purpose is to prove that he exists. The argument we first expected was:

   A. All my beliefs are false. (*hypothesis*)
      It follows that I exist.
      That I exist is one of my beliefs.
      Therefore not all my beliefs can be false. (*the hypothesis fails*)

This argument was never carried through, for Descartes seemed to become interested in asserting his existence in the course of it and apparently substitutes the following:

   B. All my beliefs are false. (*hypothesis*)
      Therefore I exist.

But this is clearly invalid. Supposing that his existence does follow from the hypothesis, it is illegitimate to assert something as proved which follows from a premise that is only hypothetical. Moreover, since the assertion of his existence is presumably incompatible with the assertion that all his beliefs are false, his existence should be reason to reject the premise and throw out the argument. And bring us back to the beginning again.

Sometimes Descartes speaks as if he means the argument to go as follows:

   C. I am trying to suppose that all my beliefs are false.
      From this it follows that I exist.
      Therefore I exist.[12]

This argument, in contrast to the first two, has an assertive premise rather than a hypothetical one. It loses the advantage therefore of being an argument that depends on nothing else being known. The hypothetical form fits Descartes's original

12. I believe this roughly represents the form of Descartes's statement, "Of a surety I myself did exist since I persuaded myself of something . . ." (H.R., II, 150), translated it into the present tense.

project, to start his philosophy from the barest beginning. But this one depends upon the truth of the premise that he is trying to suppose a particular thing, a premise which on its face might be false. He might, that is, be deluding himself or doing something different. And it is not a good reply to say that it doesn't matter what Descartes is doing, that whatever he is doing (supposing, daydreaming, and the like) will afford just as good a premise as the premise that he is supposing everything false. For such a defense says that any of a number of arguments *would be* good arguments, depending on which premise is true; but it fails to tell us *which* argument is the basis for Descartes's conclusion that he exists.[13] Whatever his argument is here, it has a premise that either is or is not true. And while its truth may not worry Descartes, who is engaged in a soliloquy, it worries anyone who considers whether this argument is sound as an argument, whether it is a secure cornerstone of Descartes's philosophy. Again, it would not be a good defense to say that we can all mimic Descartes's procedure and, through our own meditation, find a premise to prove our own existence. Our existence is not the conclusion Descartes sets out to prove. In sum, Descartes is faced with a dilemma: the argument that he exists, standing as it does at the very beginning of his system, should have a hypothetical pre-

---

13. Could there be an argument that comprehends all the alternative premises which referred to thinking in Descartes's broad sense? Could there be an argument, that is, which went like this?

> Either I am doubting or hypothesizing or reasoning or imagining. . . .
> If I am either doubting or hypothesizing or reasoning or imagining . . . then I exist.
> Therefore I exist.

If there is, perhaps this would solve the problem of the uncertain premise. But it would be much less convincing than *cogito ergo sum,* being so very odd and cumbersome.

mise and form; but from such an argument the conclusion that he exists cannot be drawn.

Descartes sometimes suggests that his argument has this form:

> D. All my beliefs are false. (*hypothesis*)
> As I consider this, I must exist.
> Therefore, inasmuch as (or whenever) I think, I exist.

This argument is very curious. The hypothetical premise does not support the conclusion or have any logical connection with it except in providing the occasion for asserting it. The conclusion is a general statement or principle. By no means could it derive from a hypothesis without being itself hypothetical. Nor could it derive from the hypothesis in conjunction with a proposition about Descartes's present existence. The conclusion might as well have been asserted barely, by itself, on the occasion of Descartes's meditation.

Descartes gives yet one more account of how the conclusion that he exists is obtained. It seems inspired by the fact that the conclusion of argument D appeared to need a more general premise about everything which thinks, a premise for which Descartes has no warrant. He writes:

He who says '*I think, hence I am or exist*' does not deduce existence from thought by a syllogism, but, by a simple act of mental vision recognizes it as if it were a thing known *per se*. This is evident from the fact that if it were syllogistically deduced, the major premise, *that everything that thinks is, or exists*, would have to be known previously.[14]

Descartes says he recognizes that he exists by a 'simple act of mental vision.' Is this all there is to knowing that he exists? Descartes doesn't satisfy us on the point. He says we recognize it *as if* it were known *per se* or of itself; does that mean

14. H.R., II, 38.

it is so known or not?[15] We have no way to answer. If it is known *per se*, then no argument was ever necessary. He needed only to arrive at this vision.

The question which strikes us now is whether Descartes ever really wanted to prove his existence. The question is inevitable, as we view the confusion with which he surrounded his discussions of the proof. Also, if he had wanted a valid argument for his existence, he could have constructed one easily. He could have used the simple constructive dilemma

> E. If all my beliefs are false, I exist.
>
> If not all my beliefs are false, I exist.
>
> Either all my beliefs are false or they are not.
>
> Therefore I exist.[16]

This argument avoids both the problems of the argument by hypothesis (which doesn't yield the conclusion that he exists) and the problem of the soliloquy (which rests on an unproved contingent premise). It also avoids the need for a general principle and its alternative, the 'act of mental vision.' Why didn't Descartes use this?

Descartes's intentions in the Second Meditation are not clear and are never openly shared with his readers. It is troubling that he does not always take his own explanations seriously: if he meant that there is no inference but an act of mental vision, why did he not contradict Hobbes and Gassendi when they spoke of the 'inference' he makes from thinking to existing?[17] It almost seems that he was not interested in this proof, that it was unimportant to him. But it was important, surely, if it was the beginning upon which our other

---

15. Willis Doney called my attention to the importance of "as if" in this passage, which secures it against unequivocal interpretation.

16. Peter Kissin pointed this out to me.

17. Hobbes wrote: "It is quite certain that the knowledge of this proposition, *I exist*, depends upon that other one, *I think*, as he [Descartes] has correctly shown us. But whence comes our knowledge of this proposition, *I think*?" (H.R., II, 62).

knowledge depends, and from which other arguments were to flow.[18] Let us address in a general way the task Descartes ostensibly set himself—the task of proving that he exists.

2

That one exists follows from a multitude of propositions about oneself. That I exist follows from the proposition that my shoes are too tight, and from the proposition that my cousin lives nearby, and from the proposition that I feel depressed, and from the proposition that I am late to class. These are very common things to assert, and only a few of the great number I may assert in a day, all of which entail that I exist. It should be very easy to give a proof of one's existence, then, if what is needed is to assert a true proposition from which one's existence follows. But is this what is needed?

Besides the availability of premises from which the conclusion follows, another matter needs to be considered regarding a proof that one exists. The question is: Is it sufficient for the proving of a proposition—and for inferring it—that it be deducible from another proposition which we truly assert? The question has these instances: If a line contains an infinite number of points, can we infer that it has eight? If we know something is a man, can we infer that it is human? The question I raise is a question about the meaning of 'inference' and the notion of 'proof.'

Gassendi questioned Descartes about his argument, asking why he "needed all that mechanism" regarding the premise 'I think' when "our natural light informs us that whatever acts also exists."[19] He calls attention to the ease with which he can prove he exists, if what is desired is merely a true premise from which that follows. Anything we do establishes our

18. See the Appendix of this chapter for my explanation why Descartes should so neglect this important argument.
19. H.R., II, 137.

existence. The question is not whether we have such premises, but whether we can use them to prove our existence.

The most common form of objection to such an argument is the charge of *petitio principii* or circularity. For if one knows the premise 'I think' (or 'I walk,' and so forth), one knows that one exists without occasion to infer it. But what sort of objection is this? Suppose Descartes's proof is circular. That doesn't mean it is invalid: on the contrary it must be valid if it is circular. Nothing is formally wrong with it.[20] Circular arguments are commonly classed as 'fallacious' for reasons independent of their validity, for reasons having to do with what might be termed their use. For they cannot persuade someone of their purported conclusion, provided he understands the premises. They cannot carry someone from the admission that the premises are true to the acceptance of the conclusion. They fail therefore to serve one of the principal functions of arguments. A person presenting such an argument does so from ignorance or trickery; a person accepting one does so through misunderstanding. In that case, should we speak of an 'inference' embodied in the argument? Should we speak here of a 'proof'?

In mathematics we are familiar with proofs given of things about which people do not differ, things no one questions. For instance, a proof could be given that opposite angles are equal (which anyone can see!), or that whatever is a natural number has a successor. No one who understands the subject of these proofs is persuaded by them. They are lacking in power to persuade someone that the conclusion is true. No one accepts the conclusions because of the proofs. And in this respect such 'proofs' lack efficacy. They are like circular ar-

20. Hintikka argues, using an analogy, that the argument is invalid because it is a *petitio principii*. That this is a mistake and that both the *cogito* and the argument Hintikka presents are valid is shown by Kenny (*op. cit.*, p. 61).

guments. In one important sense of 'inference' they do not involve inference.

I am proposing that in an important sense there is no inference from there being infinitely many points on a line to there being eight. There is in this sense no inference from someone's being a man to his being human. And there is no inference from my thinking to my existence. Finally, there is no inference, in this sense, from any premise about myself to the conclusion that I exist.

Philosophers writing about Descartes's argument have neglected this point. Malcolm, for one, writes: "It is not difficult to understand Descartes's conviction that . . . he had proved his own existence with certainty."[21] Surely Malcolm means that Descartes has proved it against his inclination to doubt, has reached certainty about his existence by means of this argument. But a circular argument cannot persuade him. Then should we say merely that Descartes gives a valid argument for his existence? But this claim is trivial.

Harry Frankfurt, in his discussion of Descartes's argument, is more cautious. He writes: "The permanent availability of *sum* rests upon its derivability from a premiss that is necessarily available whenever it is needed."[22] He implies that he thinks such a premise might be needed. But is this a serious possibility? Frankfurt thinks it is:

Even without claiming that he can be certain of whether he is thinking or of whether he is considering *sum*, therefore, Descartes can properly maintain that a premiss entailing *sum* can never be lacking *on an occasion when the reasonableness of asserting* sum *becomes a question.*[23]

21. "Descartes's Proof that His Essence is Thinking" (in W. Doney, ed., p. 312).
22. *Op. cit.*, p. 111.
23. *Ibid.*, p. 112. The italics are mine.

But what kind of occasion is it when such a question arises? Let us try to imagine one: A person is half-conscious and dazed, concerned with his state. He asks to be spoken to and asks if he is still alive. He reaches out, touches objects nearby. Then he exclaims, "I'm alive—I exist!" In this uncommon case would we say that such a person had proved to himself that he exists? Not, certainly, in the sense of proving a proposition from premises. It is incongruous to suppose that what such a person needed was a premise from which his existence could be *inferred* by him! Yet if such an occasion as this is not one where the "reasonableness of asserting *sum* becomes a question," how are we to find one?

Frankfurt would surely answer that philosophers concerned with a proof of their existence were not interested in examples like that above. By occasions when asserting *sum* is reasonable, they have meant philosophical occasions. Frankfurt means that philosophers are entitled to assert *sum* in the course of their enquiries.[24] But without an ordinary, common-sense interpretation of this 'need,' the appeal of Descartes's procedure is lost. The obscurity of the need to assert *sum* lends obscurity to his enterprise.

We have found that it is very easy to find propositions from which our existence can be deduced. They are ubiquitous—they are asserted every day. But it is extremely hard to find an appropriate use for 'I exist.' While we can with ingenuity find one, the one we find will not serve philosophically. A philosopher is not, for example, in a dazed or semiconscious state, and presumably has no anxiety over his condition. His situation, at work in his study, is no background for asserting that he exists. So while there are plenty of premises for one's existence, no setting is provided for a proof; and this is so partly because of the extreme rarity of occasions when asserting 'I

24. *Ibid.*, pp. 107ff.

exist' makes sense. We need further to understand why a philosopher might think that 'I exist' should be provable, but not 'provable' in the formal sense of giving a deductive proof nor in a sense in which proof is occasioned by doubt.[25]

25. Hintikka wrestles with this problem and argues that *cogito ergo sum* is best understood as a 'performance' and not as an inference. He writes: "The function of the word *cogito* in Descartes' dictum is to refer to the thought-act through which the existential self-verifiability of 'I exist' manifests itself" (*op. cit.*, p. 122). He follows Descartes's suggestion that what proves he exists is the process, the act, of thinking. Hintikka refers to the act of thinking through which one's existence becomes known to one as a "performance" (pp. 110, 118). He explains that Descartes discovers the "self-verifiability" of *sum* "is indubitable *because* and *in so far as* it is actively thought of" (p. 122). *Sum* depends on *cogito*, but not in the way that a conclusion depends upon a premise: "In Descartes' argument the relation of *cogito* to *sum* is not that of a premise to a conclusion. Their relation is rather comparable with that of a *process* to its *product*. The indubitability of my own existence results from my thinking of it almost as the sound of music results from playing it or (to use Descartes' own metaphor) light in the sense of illumination (*lux*) results from the presence of a source of light (*lumen*)" (p. 122). The conclusion *sum* emanates from thinking, and *cogito* "refers to the 'performance' (to the act of thinking) through which the sentence 'I exist' may be said to verify itself . . . , an attempt to think in the sense of making myself believe . . . that I do not exist" (p. 123). 'I exist' is incapable of being thought false; just to think it is to verify that it is true. It is, in Hintikka's words, "existentially self-verifying." Conversely, 'I don't exist' is incapable of being thought true; it is "existentially self-defeating." The act of thinking or uttering these sentences is sufficient for their verification or falsification, respectively. Hintikka's account has the virtue of interpreting Descartes's remarks about knowing that he exists by an 'act of mental vision,' so these are reconciled with his giving a 'proof' of his existence. It further explains why Descartes's insists that his premise should involve some 'verb of intellection' and not 'walk,' for instance (p. 139). His account is nonetheless vulnerable to the objections raised against Frankfurt's account and Descartes's own statement: Inasmuch as it is proof, it must be related to a context where a proof might be effective, where it might reassure or persuade. And

3

As we see, 'I exist' is rarely used and belongs in circumstances that are unusual, even bizarre. Why then do we think of it as a common—even omnipresent—truth? Why does it seem an everyday and familiar one? The source of this idea is the same for us as it was for Descartes: we think that among the sum collection of our beliefs must be counted a belief that we exist.

'I exist' is surely a good sentence. But what assures us that it expresses a belief? Why should we think we have a belief that we exist? There is an argument that supports this idea: Many of the things we assert—and by asserting express our beliefs—entail that we exist. My existence follows from my having lost a sock, having an ill-fitting shoe, having no money in the bank, and so on. Countless sentences in everyday currency express beliefs and also entail that the speaker exists. Each time someone uses one of them to express a belief, his existence is strictly implied. Then how can one's existence not be a belief, one most commonly expressed by such implications? This is why 'I exist' seems such a familiar truth. It is

---

precisely this cannot be done. There is no role for Hintikka's performative proof any more than for the formal demonstration. It is a philosophical invention that has no function.

An analogous argument can be made against the entire concept of self-verification and its opposite, self-defeat. Although Hintikka first explains these concepts in connection with *utterances* or *statements*, it is soon apparent that their chief application is to sentences that no one utters. There are no utterances of 'I exist' which make sense in the philosophical context, and so none to be self-verifying. The idea of 'proof' by this means is vacuous. One might go further and argue that it is precisely the features which make a sentence 'self-verifying' which also make it useless for philosophical inquiry. Hintikka lamely insists that these sentences are, however unusable, "perfectly correct as sentences" (p. 118). But their 'perfect correctness' entails nothing about their meaning or its limitations; nor should it lead us to think they can be proved.

entailed by so many common belief-expressing sentences that we are bound to conclude it expresses a belief as well. We certainly cannot reasonably doubt or deny it! But now, if it is a belief, we can surely ask what might prove its truth.

This line of reasoning is persuasive. It is so because the following assumption seems self-evident: If we assert a proposition expressing a belief and that proposition entails another, then the latter must represent one of our beliefs too. On this assumption, if I say that my friend S is in town (expressing my belief), then any propositions entailed by this proposition would also express my belief. If it is entailed that S is a person and S is alive and that S is my friend, then each of these propositions represents a belief of mine as much as the one I asserted.[26]

Although many philosophers have treated this assumption as self-evident, it is not very difficult to see that it is false. And if it is false, then justification is lacking for saying that there is a ubiquitous belief that we exist. And if there is no such common belief, then there is no need to prove that it is true. Descartes's curious attempt to prove his existence was then also unnecessary.

How can we discover if such a principle is true? Consider this example: Suppose a person says he has two dollars, expressing his belief that he has two dollars. Can we infer that he believes he has one dollar? Can we make this inference about his belief *solely* on the ground that having two dollars necessitates having one? If we believe what he says, we infer that he has one dollar; that is not the question. The question is whether *his believing* he has one dollar follows from *his believing* that he has two? Another way to ask the question is to ask: Does entailment between beliefs follow the pattern of entailment between propositions expressing beliefs?

Consider the example above. Suppose, having heard that

26. See, for instance, Hintikka's *Knowledge and Belief*, Ch. 2.

speaker say he has two dollars, I report to a third party that he believes he has one dollar. Might the speaker not contradict me, saying that is not his belief? He says he *said* he had two dollars, and that is what he meant. If he had meant that he had one, he would have said that instead. I don't think I could insist that he *must* have believed he had one dollar because he believed he had two. His belief is not governed by such a 'must.'

Or imagine this situation. Someone asserts that it's raining. From his assertion it follows that the humidity is high. May I then report that the speaker believed that the humidity is high? We can easily imagine him protesting that I am twisting his words, that *that* was not his belief. He said it was raining, and if he had meant that the humidity is high he would have said *that*! It was his choice what to say and so what to express. We cannot infer what beliefs he must have by this simple use of propositional relations.

I do not imply that people may or do deny the consequences of what they assert. If they did they would be subject to the charge of inconsistency. A person who asserts that he has two dollars will not deny that he has one; a person who remarks that it is raining will not deny that the humidity is high. But what follows from this? It would be foolish to infer that *therefore* a person has beliefs concerning these things. The following examples help make clear the distinction between having a belief and accepting something. A person may hold and may assert that all men are mortal, and from this it follows that men whom he does not know are mortal. It follows, for example, that someone actually living in Asia with an Asian name in an Asian town will die. But it plainly does not follow that the speaker *believed* that this person will die, although the speaker will surely concede that any particular person is mortal. Again, someone may assert that a property holds of all natural numbers. And it follows from this that the property holds of a number larger than any anyone has thought of. But it clearly is false that the speaker *believes* that that particular number has the property, while he would surely agree that any number, including that one, must have it.

My account of belief does not conflict with the practice of argument, therefore, the practice according to which a person may be forced by entailment to accept something he would otherwise deny. But it does conflict with the assumption that accepting a proposition is the same as having a belief. A question about what someone believes cannot be settled by a deduction; it must be referred to the person. One might say: beliefs are discrete. They are not hooked together in chains. The argument for thinking they are rests on the assumption that the objects of beliefs are propositions (which *are* conceived to be hooked together) and the assumption that what holds of the objects of belief must hold of beliefs as well—both of which are false. The grammar of belief-expression is not the grammar of propositional logic.

If it is no longer clear that we must have a belief that we exist, then it is implausible that we normally have such a belief. When would we express it? When would we doubt whether it was so? When would we look for proof, and what would it be to find it? In normal circumstances we have no place for such a 'belief,' while in those extraordinary circumstances where one asks, 'Do I exist?', giving a proof with its premises is incongruous. The alternative to saying that we always have such a belief, that it is omnipresent, presupposed, unconscious, or instinctive, is to say that we very rarely or never have it, that it is an odd and curious thing and has no everyday characteristic expression. But without such expression our attention cannot be focused on such a belief. Without characteristic expression the 'belief' becomes shapeless and part of the background against which genuine beliefs are expressed. As it thus escapes our field of vision, the 'belief' becomes more clearly an imaginary thing. There is ordinarily no such belief.

Let me make clear that denying that there is a belief that we

exist is not the same as affirming that we *dis*believe or doubt
that we exist. On the contrary, I am arguing that 'I exist' is
not a common belief-expressing sentence, and therefore doubting and disbelieving that we exist have no more philosophical
substance than the 'belief' does. There is neither a belief nor
a disbelief that we exist; therefore we do not have to choose
which has the better claim to our support.

There is no common belief that we exist, but that is not a
sign of our irrationality. The belief that we exist does not
stand at the beginning of the system which constitutes our
knowledge, for there is no such belief. But without such a
belief it seems unlikely that there is such a 'system' with a
logical 'beginning.' The Cartesian effort to begin philosophy
and a defense of knowledge this way was a mistake.

Looking back on Descartes's first hypothesis—that all his
beliefs were false—which the assertion 'I exist' seemed to de-
feat, what can we say of it? If the famous exception to the
possibility that all his beliefs were false fails, if there is no belief that he exists, does this mean that the hypothesis holds? Is
it possible that all his—or our—beliefs may be false? Such a
possibility requires a class of beliefs of course. But how is this
class to be conceived? Is it to be collected of many different
situations and all the varieties of uses of 'I believe' together
with other expressions of belief? But these will not be consistent any more than the contexts for saying one knows are.
Moreover, there is no expression of belief which is context-
independent, just as there is no use of 'I know' with this feature. In short, we have no way of constructing the required
class. Like the class of all that one knows, the class of all one
believes is a philosophical fiction.

Nevertheless, the temptation to speak of such a class persists
by way of the following inference: If you assert (and believe)
a thing at one time, and have afterwards no reason to think the
situation has changed, then your belief persists until some
change occurs or the matter is forgotten. Accordingly, if to-

day you say, "My check has gone to the bank by now," expressing your belief about your check, then tomorrow this belief will still be there unchanged, and will stay there unless some circumstance arises to change it. But is this description right? Does your belief remain until the end of the month, for example? Does it persist until the end of the year? Or indefinitely? Do you have such a belief for every pay check unless perchance one check is forgotten? For example, "I believe February's and March's and May's of 1956 have been deposited, but I find no belief about April's." This strikes me as absurd. Even should someone ask you two weeks after payday if you still believed your check had been deposited you might be bewildered. What, you would wonder, has happened to occasion this question? The question doesn't ring the same now as it would have before. And you would certainly not answer, "Oh yes, the same old belief is there!" In a similar way we do not have continuing beliefs that last winter is gone or that we survived the first year of life.[27] A belief belongs in a context where its expression makes sense.

But now, is this not to limit the *having* of a belief to the *expressing* of it? And such an interpretation is surely too narrow. Beliefs endure; they continue past the moment of their expression. But are these remarks not metaphorical? Do they really mean that beliefs are entities which are stored? To be sure, some examples suggest this picture. For instance, we may ask someone if he still believes that Wallace will run for president, and he might ponder a moment or so, then say that yes, he still believes it, as he has for the last four years. While he is pondering, it seems as if he were searching to see if that belief was still among his store; and his answer seems to mean that he has found it. But this picture only fits some few beliefs. It doesn't fit the beliefs about pay checks, for their expression is

27. Other such 'continuing but unexpressed beliefs' will be treated in the next chapter, where we consider the 'beliefs' of common sense.

appropriate for only a short interval. Two weeks is too long normally for the continuation of a belief that my pay check has been deposited, but it is not too long for the belief that Aunt Thelma will answer my letter. The interval within which a belief might be expressed is determined partly by the nature of the belief, the matter believed. What is true of one will not be true of others. And it is partly determined by the context of its expression. Therefore, the storehouse picture and the implication that beliefs are storable entities is a generalization from the way we treat certain instances of belief; it is false taken of beliefs in general, and for some it is absurd.

I conclude then that there is no class of 'all the things one believes' as Descartes requires there be. Therefore 'I exist' cannot be a member of such a class. Nor is there any such 'hypothesis' as the hypothesis that all the members of that class are false. The class is as much a fiction as the class of 'all the things one knows.' The phrase 'everything one believes' has a use to be sure. But it is a particular one, specialized as much as the use of 'everything one knows' was found to be. It follows that Descartes's procedure and the doubt with which he thought philosophy should begin were misconceived.

The assumption that there are many unexpressed beliefs which we must have because we have certain beliefs of ordinary kinds, expressed in ordinary situations, is an assumption we will discuss again in the next chapter. It is perhaps one of the most troublesome assumptions in the philosophy of knowledge, and has helped to shape wrongly our idea of what the philosophy of knowledge should be.

4

We have considered the Cartesian idea that there is a primitive belief that we exist and that it is provable. By studying the various forms of proof Descartes gives or suggests, we came to question the point of giving one. We found that 'I exist' is easy enough to derive if what is needed is a premise from which it follows. Our daily speech is embarrassingly rich in such premises. Where then is the difficulty of giving a proof? First, such proofs are circular, and this means they cannot answer a genuine doubt. But second, there is no doubt which such a proof could answer. While 'I exist' may have a use, and 'Do I exist?' may also, a formal proof that one exists will not answer any such question. The 'proof' lacks a function.

If no proof effectively proves that we exist, is that belief without ground? But what assures us there is such a belief? It cannot be just assumed. There is a justification for it, employing the assumption that if a proposition is entailed by some other proposition which expresses belief, then the former expresses our belief too. This assumption is false, I argued. The logical connections which bind propositions do not bind beliefs. Beliefs relate to their appropriate expression, and so to appropriate circumstances, and these are not determined by the connections between sentences.

Without this assumption we can see there is no belief that we exist and no place for a proof of it. The Cartesian enterprise is seen to be misconceived; the easy steps of Descartes's argument have led us wrong. For the picture of belief inherent in that enterprise neglects the fact that some sentences of a contingent kind do not express beliefs while others, standing in the closest logical relation to them, do.

In the next chapter we shall employ some similar reasoning with respect to other propositions which, though they seem to express beliefs of a very fundamental kind—though it even seems they *must* do so—really do not. Such propositions, like 'I exist' are among the most fascinating and puzzling in philosophy.[28]

28. I am very grateful for help given me on this chapter by Willis Doney and Harry Frankfurt, with both of whom I respectfully disagree.

Appendix

Having shown that Descartes's hypothesis was misconceived and that there is no such belief as the belief that one exists, I turn to the curious way Descartes proceeds, vacillating in his statement of the proof that he exists and with each new explanation clouding further what significance that proof is supposed to have. I wish to put forward a hypothesis to explain these strange maneuvers.

No sooner does Descartes present his proof that he exists than he asks, even in the same breath, what sort of being he is. In this way he encourages his reader to think there is a very close connection between the proof that he exists and the claim that he is a thinking thing—a thing whose nature is to think.[29] But just what is the connection? Descartes sometimes suggests it is logical, as when he writes in the Second Meditation

What of thinking? I find here that thought is an attribute that belongs to me; it alone cannot be separated from me. I am, I exist, that is certain. But how often? Just when I think; for it might possibly be the case if I ceased entirely to think, that I should likewise cease altogether to exist. I do not now admit anything which is not necessarily true. . . . I am a real thing and really exist; but what thing? I have answered: a thing which thinks.[30]

One is taken aback when Descartes asks 'But how often?' Why should he ask that? His answer reveals his purpose: he wants to assert that thinking is the mark, the assurance of his existence. And from *this* he will conclude that he is essentially a thing which thinks.

29. E.g., Malcolm gives a detailed argument showing that Descartes used the *cogito* as a foundation for his *sum res cogitans* proof. Frankfurt, on the other hand, proposes that the two arguments are continuous, even one, though he fails to convince us why Descartes should make them appears so (*op. cit.* Ch. 11).

30. H.R., I, 151–152,

Thinking, which includes doubting and setting hypotheses, is surely connected with knowing that he exists. For if he is aware of his existence he must necessarily be thinking. There is then a logical connection between *knowing that he exists* and being conscious, which is to say, *thinking*. But is there such a necessary connection between *existing* and being aware or *thinking?* This is not at all evident. But that is the connection Descartes is pressed to establish. He wants to show that he *must* be a thinking thing because of his proof that he exists.

The implausibility of this inference did not escape Descartes, I conjecture. He must have seen that stating it baldly would have provoked criticism. Therefore he returns again and again to reformulate the proof of his existence: I think, so I am; and inasmuch as I think, I am; and whenever I think, I am assured that I am. This shows, does it not, that there is a vital and even a necessary connection between thinking and existing? It does not of course! It would show at best that there is a connection between thinking and knowing that he exists. But it does not show that he must be a thing which thinks. It does not show that he is necessarily a thinking thing.

Descartes was faced with a dilemma here. On the one hand he could easily 'prove' that he existed. He could have done this without any prior assumption or assertion, for he could proceed with a simple constructive dilemma had he chosen. In any case he could have presented his proof that he exists clearly and unequivocally. But supposing this conclusion is established, where could he proceed then? What follows from his existence alone? If this was to be the fixed point which made possible great advances, how was that to be shown? It could not be. That he exists is a conclusion barren of further consequences. It is a fixed point which makes nothing else possible. Therefore Descartes was forced to return to the proof that he exists and try to establish there the connection which would make plausible the further claim that he is a thinking thing. In doing this, by necessity he muddies the argument for his existence. In a sense this is his purpose. He does not want to correct Hobbes and Mersenne about their interpretations of the 'inference' that he exists, nor does he wish to spell out whether an inference is involved here or an 'act of mental vision.' What he needs is emphasis on the close connection between thinking and existing: the 'simple act of mental vision' suggests that it is very close indeed. Furthermore there was no reason to defend the argument for his existence, because this was of all his arguments the least vulnerable to contemporary criticism. Therefore Descartes used that argument to help him prove that he must be a thing which thinks. He was very little concerned with its virtues as a proof of his existence, as a proof in its own right.

On this conjecture we can explain some curiousities connected with the proof that Descartes exists. It explains why he rejects as premises for his existence such propositions as 'I walk' or 'I eat.' These do not call attention to the central place of thinking, and it is of less concern to him that he have a premise for his existence which is indubitable than that he should have a vehicle for persuading us that he is essentially a thinking thing.

I propose that the argument for his existence, as Descartes states it in the Second Meditation and defends it and interprets it in other places, is a fraud, and that its real purpose was to allow Descartes to prove that he is a thinking thing. This is not to charge Descartes with being clearly aware of this situation; speculation about how he viewed his own curious statements about the *cogito* would be chancy. What I suggest is rather that he was never seriously concerned to give a good proof of his existence and never thought proving his existence was a matter of great importance. This view of Descartes's intentions squares with my view that there is no such thing as a proof that one exists, not in the relevant sense of 'proof.' In one sense, that explains why Descartes never meant to prove it. The argument for his existence, viewed by many philosophers as the most secure in the philosophy of knowledge, is then a piece of deception. It is the 'first proposition' in the structure of knowledge only in the sense of providing a connection between ones thinking and ones existence, which Descartes will need subsequently.

On this interpretation, the proof of his existence and the proof that he is a thinking thing can be viewed as continuous. They are one complex argument.[31] Their being joined in the Second Meditation serves to help persuade us that they are inseparable. Indeed the question whether there is an inference from thinking to existence leads to the question whether one's existence and one's thinking are separate ideas; if they are, then by Descartes's own doctrine they must be separable in reality as well.[32] And then where is the *necessity* that he be a thing which thinks? The 'inference' from thinking to existence is, on this view, more safely replaced by a 'simple act of mental vision,' with no gap to be bridged and no separation to be explained.

31. Frankfurt raises the question why, in a later passage concerned with the criterion of clearness and distinctness, Descartes speaks of his "first cognition" as the knowledge that he is a thinking thing rather than *sum* (*op. cit.*, p. 114). He remarks that Descartes does this because of the "very close relationship he conceives to hold between the statement that he is a thinking thing, and the statement *sum* as it occurs in his proof that his existence is certain" (p. 114). Frankfurt claims that Descartes "presents the statement that he is a thinking thing as nothing more than an explicit rendering of *sum*," and that Descartes is inclined to treat the two statements as "interchangeable" (pp. 114–115). What Frankfurt doesn't tell us is why Descartes should do this. The reason is that Descartes needs to treat the *cogito* as showing that his essence is thought or he will not have any argument for that claim. The confusion generated has an important function: it leads us from doubting our beliefs to the conclusion that we are necessarily thinking things.

32. The principle that what is inseparable in thought is inseparable in reality is made to apply to the connection between his existence and his essence in Meditation VI (H.R., I, 190).

Viewing the two proofs as one also explains another curious fact—that Descartes refers to his conclusion that he is a thinking thing as his 'first knowledge'.[33] For insofar he separates the proof of his existence from the proof that he must be a thinking thing, the force of the latter is lost. His first cognition must be both proofs seen as one.

33. H.R., I, 158.

VI

Common-Sense Beliefs

Moore once characterized his philosophical position by saying that he was one of the philosophers "who have held that the 'Common Sense view of the world' is, in certain fundamental features, *wholly* true."[1] Among the features of that view were: that the world has existed for many years, that time is real, that space is real, that there are material things, and that there are other humans with their own beliefs and feelings.[2] Moore's reaction to any denial of these things was vehement. He once said that 'Time is unreal' seemed to him "a perfectly monstrous proposition" and he did his best to argue against it.[3]

Moore's argument against those opposed to the common-sense view was two-sided. Against those who denied it altogether he argued *ad hominem* that such denial was self-con-

1. "A Defence of Common Sense," *Philosophical Papers*, p. 44 (hereafter in this chapter referred to as 'DCS').
2. *Ibid.*, pp. 33, 39.
3. "An Autobiography," in Schilpp, ed., *The Philosophy of G. E. Moore*, p. 14.

tradictory, for the assertion that there *is* such a view entails that parts of it are true. The assertion that there is such a view entails, for one thing, that there are human beings holding those beliefs. Second, he argued that certain features of the common-sense view were simply *true*. He argued, for instance, that time and space are real and material things exist. This second part of Moore's defense of common sense' will concern me here.

Of the practical importance of proving that time is real, Moore once wrote:

It is, no doubt, immensely important that we should all have beliefs with regard to the temporal relations of particular things. An enormous number of our actions are guided by such beliefs. So that if the adoption of the philosophic creed that there is no such thing as Time led us to abandon all such beliefs in ordinary life, it would be of immense practical importance which creed, upon this point, we did adopt. But I think there is no danger whatever that any philosopher, however sincerely he may adopt the philosophic opinion that there is no such thing as Time, will ever be able to divest himself of particular beliefs which contradict this opinion.[4]

In their everyday affairs everyone accepts the reality of time, Moore believed, even philosophers who denied it. Nevertheless he thought the philosophical denial of it needed an answer: the truth of that denial has consequences for the truth of the Common Sense view, and whether anyone acts on those consequences or not, the Common Sense view should be defended against attack, Moore thought.

My discussion of Moore's defense of Common Sense follows this plan: first I consider Moore's argument in favor of the proposition 'Time is real'; second I consider how his argument is related to those of his opponents James McTaggart

4. *Some Main Problems of Philosophy* (London: Allen and Unwin, 1953), p. 203 (hereafter in this chapter referred to as *SMPP*).

and F. H. Bradley; last I raise some questions about the kinds of inferences employed by the parties to this philosophical disagreement.

1

In "A Defence of Common Sense," Moore gave a list of 'truisms' he claimed to know with certainty. While his list made references to himself, his body, and the objects and events around him, he thought other people had similar lists of propositions about themselves and the objects around them and that they knew those propositions just as he did his.[5] His list included the proposition that the world existed for many years before he was born, the proposition that he had a body, the proposition that he had had various feelings and thoughts, and so on. Moore said he was assuming that each of these propositions had a meaning which was "*the* ordinary or popular meaning."[6] He thought they could hardly be misunderstood. Furthermore, these propositions entailed other, very general propositions, such as 'Time is real,' 'Space is real,' and 'There are material things.'[7] Moore allowed for the fact that philosophers have had somewhat different meanings in mind when they denied that time and space are real.[8] But he thought

5. Throughout this chapter I have struggled with the 'sentence-proposition-statement' terminology, which, as I have explained, it seems neither reasonable to accept nor possible to ignore. Since the issue involved here concerns what to make of the truisms—*what they are*—it is particularly important that such distinctions should not prejudice the answer. It may be helpful to use the word '*Satz*' to get the sense of some of my remarks.

6. 'DCS,' p. 36.

7. *Ibid.*, pp. 38ff.

8. No doubt Moore was thinking here of the fact that, while both McTaggart and Bradley denied the reality of time, the latter claimed that it was anyway an 'appearance.' Therefore, they interpreted the unreality of time rather differently, which means that 'Time is real' was also viewed differently by them.

there was one usage which is "the most natural and proper usage of each of these expressions"—that is, 'Time is real,' 'Space is real'—and that denying them in this usage conflicted with his truisms and so with the Common Sense view.[9] He reasonably inferred that the denial of these propositions was *intended* to contradict that view.[10]

Moore went to great pains to explain how expressions like 'Time is unreal' should be understood. His explanation was indeed part of his argument against them:

So long as [a philosophical view] is merely presented in vague phrases such as: All that we know of material objects is the orderly succession of our own sensations; it does, in fact, sound very plausible. But, so soon as you realize what it means in particular instances like that of the train—how it means that you cannot possibly know that your carriage is, even probably, running on wheels, or coupled to other carriages—it seems to me to lose all its plausibility.[11]

A view abstractly stated may be plausible, but it loses plausibility when its consequences are expressed concretely. Moore describes this procedure in regard to 'Time is unreal.'

If you try to translate the proposition into the concrete and to ask what it *implies*, there is, I think, very little doubt as to the sort of thing it implies.[12]

What does it imply? In another place he spells it out:

[This view] holds . . . that there is not really any such thing as Time at all; that nothing whatever really exists or happens *in* Time; and that, if, therefore, anybody believes that anything whatever happened before or after anything else, or that any two

9. *Ibid.*, p. 38.
10. *Ibid.*, p. 39.
11. *SMPP*, p. 135.
12. *Philosophical Studies* (London: Routledge and Kegan Paul, 1948), p. 209 (hereafter in this chapter referred to as *PS*). Italics are Moore's.

events ever happened at the same time, or that any one thing ever lasted longer than another, or that anything has existed in the past or is existing now or will exist in the future, he is simply making a mistake, because, in fact, *all* such beliefs are false.[13]

If time is unreal, then all the beliefs we express regarding events and temporal intervals, the past and the future, are false beliefs. It would be false for me to assert now that it is noon, although the clock shows both hands at twelve and the bell is sounding twelve and I have no reason to think that they are wrong. It would be false as well for me to say that it has been raining for half an hour, or even that it's raining now. All remarks like these would be false and the beliefs expressed would be mistaken, and their being false and mistaken would follow simply as the consequence of a philosophical view.

Even though 'Time is unreal' is ambiguous, Moore is saying, its meaning is clear enough in this respect: it entails the falsity of all the things we assert and all the things we believe about events happening and things enduring. And when such consequences are put baldly, the view loses some plausibility. It loses plausibility by flatly contradicting an enormous number of things we ordinarily assert and believe to be true. Such loss of plausibility, however, is not a refutation of the view. How can Moore establish further that 'Time is unreal' is false?

Moore asserted that he knew his truisms to be true. And they entail together that time and space and material things are real. Therefore it seems Moore intends to *infer* from the truisms that time and space and material things are real. Conversely if an abstract proposition can be shown to contradict ordinary things which Moore is ready to say he knows, Moore would have grounds for saying that such a proposition is false.

Moore's proof that time and space and material things are real proceeds then as follows: (1) explication of the consequences of denying their reality, and (2) assertion that he

13. *SMPP*, p. 201; Moore's italics. Also see *PS*, p. 210.

knows something inconsistent with that denial. It follows—or seems to follow—that he can infer from some things he knows that time, space, and material things are real.

Moore offers the truisms as things he knows and knows for certain, which entail that time and space are real. It is necessary for Moore to convince us that he does know them, therefore. Yet Moore confesses he cannot say *how* he knows:

> I think I have nothing better to say than that it seems to me that I *do* know them, with certainty. It is, indeed, obvious that in the case of most of them, I do not know them *directly;* that is to say, I only know them because, in the past, I have known to be true *other* propositions which were evidence for them. If, for instance, I do know that the earth had existed for many years before I was born, I certainly only know this because I have known other things in the past which were evidence for it. And I certainly do not know exactly what the evidence was.[14]

The truisms, like the general propositions about time and space, are known as a result of knowing some other propositions. What sort of propositions? We can make the following conjecture. If Moore had learned that in 800 there was a severe drought, he would have learned something from which it followed that the world had existed for many years. Or if he knew that his great great grandfather came from Northumberland, he would know another thing from which the long existence of the world followed. Or if he knew that hundreds of centuries ago the world passed through an ice age, he would know another thing from which it followed as well. Can propositions like these possibly be what Moore means by the "evidence" for his belief?

Without doubt many things Moore knew entailed the long existence of the world. Yet it does not appear correct to call them *evidence*. None of these things is of such a kind that one might *infer* from them the long existence of the world. The

14. 'DCS,' p. 43; Moore's italics.

relation between these propositions and the truism is different from the relation designated by 'evidence for.' The relation is better described by saying that the particular propositions *presuppose* the truism. The particular propositions presuppose the truism inasmuch as they cannot be true unless the truism is; this is not to say that one infers or could infer the latter from the former.

If the truisms are not known directly, and if they are not known on the basis of other things which are evidence for them, their being known is really curious. How can we say we know them? And yet, how can we say we don't? Of all propositions, their truth seems virtually required by us. Wittgenstein puzzled over these propositions and his remarks, albeit metaphorical, are illuminating. He said that the reason we cannot have evidence for such propositions is that they "involve our whole way of seeing nature."[15] We lack the concepts to speak of "verifying" or "having evidence" for them. They are "part of the whole picture which forms the starting-point of belief for me," Wittgenstein wrote.[16] The proposition that the world has existed for many years "gives our way of looking at things, and our researches, their form."[17] These propositions are fundamental to our thinking, and fundamental in such a way that we cannot conceivably have evidence for them. Wittgenstein's remarks often bring the term 'presupposition' to mind. But neither this term nor his remarks dispel the mystery. We cannot see what it would be to have evidence for—and hence to know—these things.

Let us try a different approach to understanding the truisms. Let W be the proposition that the world has existed for many years, and let $P_1, P_2, \ldots$ be commonly asserted propositions which entail W. Thus P_1 might be the proposition that continents have moved over the centuries, and P_2 might be the

15. *On Certainty*, 291.
16. *Ibid.*, 209.
17. *Ibid.*, 211.

proposition that King George III was incompetent, and P_3 might be the proposition that early Christians were persecuted, and so on. Each of these propositions entails that the world has long existed. And each of them might be asserted in some fairly ordinary context. Moreover, the number of such propositions is exceedingly large (supposing we can imagine such a class), and includes propositions we assert every day or nearly every day. Therefore it is an ubiquitous consequence of our everyday assertions that the world has long existed.

It is clear, however, that you would not count P_1 or P_2 or any of the P's as *evidence* that W is true. On the contrary, they seem to depend on W! How do they do this? Why is it not just as natural to say W is inferred from them? Entailment seems to give us an inference in some cases, but it gives a presupposition in others. How can this be?

There is a feature of particular interest regarding the truisms and the propositions entailing them. Among the latter are many pairs which are contradictories. That is to say, among the propositions are some pairs such that *both the proposition and its negation entail W*. Not all of them do this, nor does it seem necessary that all propositions which presuppose a given proposition should have negations which do so as well.[18]

---

18. It can be argued that, where a proposition and its contradictory each *seems to* entail a proposition (e.g., W, that appearance is deceptive), since in the usual sense, if P entails W, then if W is false, P is false; so that both P and not-P would have to be false if W were false. It is concluded that this relation cannot be one of entailment. But it seems to me, as it did to Moore and others, that W *does follow from* P and also from not-P in a nontechnical sense of 'follows from.' This shows, of course, that W is very curious and the relation as well. Speaking of 'entailment' helps bring the peculiarity to light. It should be remarked, however, that some philosophers are more cautious on this point. For example, Bas van Fraassen gives this characterization of 'presupposition': "A presupposes B if and only if A is neither true nor false unless B is true" ("Presupposition, Implication, and Self-Reference," *Journal of Philosophy*, 65 (1968), 137). This is related to

Nonetheless this aspect of the relation of the *P*'s to *W* shows why we cannot speak of inferring *W* from some *P*. For if a thing is offered as evidence, its truth is presumably relevant to the truth of the thing it is evidence for.[19] Yet in the case of some propositions entailing the truisms, their truth is irrelevant to the truth of the latter. *W* follows from not-*P* as much as it follows from *P*. The relation between the particular propositions and the truisms that follow from them cannot be characterized by 'evidence for' or 'inferible from.' Moore was mistaken that he ever possessed 'evidence' for his truisms. It is not even clear what 'evidence' for them would be.

The characteristic of being entailed both by certain propositions and by their negations belongs to most of Moore's truisms. It belongs to the truism that I have a body, for this is entailed by the proposition that my shoes are too small and

---

Strawson's use in *Introduction to Logical Theory* (esp. pp. 175–79). However, Strawson applies this term only to 'statements' which a sentence may be used to *make*; and since the sentences I am concerned with here are not used outside philosophy, the sentence-statement distinction clouds rather than clarifies the issue. One trouble with presuppositions is that they *are not* stated or asserted, while they look as if they *might be*, and with perfectly good sense. For further discussion of such propositions see Sections 3 and 4, below.

19. I owe to Georgia Bassen this interesting example: Suppose a historical question has arisen as to whether Ethelred the Unready used a fork. The appearance of either of the following in an authenticated court circular of the time would surely count as evidence that he did use a fork: 'At breakfast this morning, the King's fork was well polished.' 'At breakfast this morning, the King's fork was not well polished.' Surely if I found either of these in the circular I could say I had found evidence for the proposition that King E. used a fork. Bassen remarks that this is not really a counter example, however, since the 'evidence' here would need to be presented in a proposition like: 'Appearing in the court circular was the sentence ". . .,"' whose negation would not in turn be evidence that the king used a fork. The example raises a more serious issue—that of what sense to give to 'propositions giving evidence for other propositions.' The terminology of propositions is obviously unsuitable here and clouds the issue.

also by the proposition that they are not; it is entailed by the proposition that I have fifty cents and by the proposition that I do not. And this relation which holds between the truisms and particular propositions entailing them also holds between the metaphysical propositions about time and space and the particular propositions entailing them. For instance, from the proposition that I had breakfast before going out, it follows that time is real; but that follows also from the proposition that I *didn't* have breakfast before going out. And from the proposition that my car is in the garage, it follows that space is real; but that follows too from the proposition that my car *isn't* in the garage. Again I do not mean that *every* ordinary proposition we might assert which entails one of these metaphysical propositions has a contradictory which also entails it, but only that many of them do. And this fact helps to account for the generality of these metaphysical propositions.

Being so related to pairs of contradictory propositions, a simple constructive dilemma-proof could be given for the truisms and the propositions about space and time, just as one could be given for the proposition that I exist. But in both cases a 'proof' does not convince. It is a formality.

Neither 'inference' nor 'evidence' is involved in the relation between the truisms and the propositions entailing them. This fact helps to illuminate some of the features of the truisms. It explains why they seem to stand *above* other propositions and have the appearance of extreme generality. It also explains why they seem so secure and immune to disproof. What kind of propositions are they, then?

The logic of propositions assures us that propositions which follow from each of a contradictory pair are necessary. Does this provide a desideratum? No. It fails to because one can argue that the pairs are not true contradictories on the single ground that they 'presuppose' the proposition at issue. To use logic to decide the question either way begs the question. Then how shall we decide it? Perhaps we should consult our intuition and ask whether it is conceivable that time should not be real. Moore seems to have done this, for he wrote:

It seems to me quite clear that it *might* have been the case that Time was not real, material things not real, Space not real, selves not real. And in favour of my view that none of these things which might have been the case, *is* in fact the case, I have, I think, no better argument than simply this—namely, that all the [truisms about my body and the existence of the world] are, in fact, true.[20]

Moore thinks it is "quite clear" that time might not have been real, but he does nothing to explain what this means. How should we interpret it? From the context we might think that Moore *infers* that time is real and material things real and so forth because their being real follows from ordinary contingent things which we assert and assert truly. As, for example, 'The lamp is on the table' entails that there is a lamp and a table, so contingent propositions entail other contingent propositions and *only* them, he might have thought. But this is false, for a contingent proposition *does* sometimes entail a necessary proposition. 'This is yellow' entails for example 'Either this is yellow or it is not.' That is one way we are justified in using 'entails' as a propositional connective.

The relation which the truisms and the propositions about space and time have to ordinary propositions that entail them shows they are not ordinary contingent propositions. Nor does it help to fix our attention on the propositions themselves. If they are contingent, they are nevertheless oddly 'fundamental' to a host of other propositions. This feature was remarked by Wittgenstein, who said that although they are contingent they "stand fast for me."[21] They stand above question and proof, as most contingent or empirical propositions do not. Not all contingent propositions have the same "status,"[22] he proposed:

20. 'DCS,' pp. 41–42; Moore's italics.
21. *On Certainty*, 151–152.
22. *Ibid.*, 167.

I do not explicitly learn the propositions that stand fast for me.
I can *discover* them subsequently like the axis around which a
body rotates. This axis is not fixed in the sense that anything holds
it fast, but the movement around it determines its mobility.[23]

We don't learn the proposition that the world has long
existed. Such things we "take on trust" as children, and there-
after our trust is "backed up" by our experience.[24] They do
not stand on evidence in the usual sense and so are "groundless."[25] Wittgenstein's remarks accord to a degree with my
account of the security of the truisms: they *are* like axes
because of their relation to the innumerable pairs of propositions and their negations, whose truth or falsity leaves the truisms unaffected. The other propositions 'move around' the
truisms in the sense of being now true, now false, while the
truisms remain constant. But this still does not tell us whether
the truisms and the propositions about space and time and
material things are contingent: Might the truisms—instead of
being true and presupposed to be true—be questioned or dis-
believed or possibly even be false?

This is a very puzzling question. The truisms have their
curious certainty in virtue of their relation to other propositions, and so do the propositions about space and time and
material things. How can we bring them into question? We
cannot imagine what it would be for time to be false—our
imagination is inadequate. Wittgenstein's remark is apt: the
picture simply falls apart. But this fails to be a proof of
noncontingency.

2

Let us view the question from another side. A contingent
proposition is one, we might say, which can conceivably be
false, and it is furthermore one which is learned through ex-

23. *Ibid.*, 152; Wittgenstein's italics.
24. *Ibid.*, 159, 275—also 288.
25. *Ibid.*, 166.

perience—a proposition for which evidence might be given and against which evidence may be imagined. Its truth is *contingent upon* what we find to be the case. Thus, if the long existence of the world is contingent, it must be imaginable that the world *should have* come into existence only a short time ago and that there *would have been* evidence for that. In that case, why is it that we find it so impossible to answer the question what evidence we *have* for this proposition? Why is it that we do not have grounds for it, though we can imagine having grounds against it?

If we were considering whether it is *true* that the world has long existed, we would be considering its grounds. But we are not considering its truth. For that consideration to arise, the truism would need to express a belief, and it would be the truth of *that belief*—a possible or hypothetical or challenged belief—to which evidence would pertain. But no one has expressed such a belief, or asked whether it may be false. There is no context for giving evidence here. So there is no sense in giving any. It is only one step further to add that, *if there is no context* where there is a question of truth or right belief and therefore no point in *giving* evidence, then there is no sense to the notion of 'evidence for the proposition' at all. Indeed, this is the conclusion we found to hold earlier of propositions that do not express beliefs: the concepts of truth and evidence do not apply to them.

There is an important difference between the following two characterizations: a proposition such that one can imagine it resting upon evidence, and a proposition resting upon evidence.[26] The latter entails that the proposition express a belief,

---

26. That there are problems with the 'a priori/a posteriori' and the 'necessary/contingent' distinctions was amply demonstrated by S. Kripke in "Naming and Necessity," in G. Harman and D. Davidson, eds., *Semantics of Natural Language* (Dordrecht: Reidel, 1972), pp. 253–355. It is further important to distinguish a sense in which mere propositions, e.g. Moore's truisms, can be contingent as opposed to beliefs being contingent, i.e., resting on other beliefs.

that the evidence for it be evidence that the belief is true. But the first characterization does not entail this. There is no need to speak of such a proposition 'resting upon' anything, nor is there any reason to consider its truth. Such a characterization, I argue, fits the truisms.

We understand the truism 'The world has long existed.' We understand it because of its connection with other sentences we use to express our beliefs. We give evidence for our beliefs, contest evidence against them and sometimes change our minds about them. Yet such has never been done with the truisms. They stand apart. The only access to their meaning, indeed, is through other propositions which entail them and which themselves have currency. Now consider the feeling of surprise we have when such a proposition is made the subject of a demand for justification in philosophy! What on earth should we say in response? The first move is to ask whether it is supposed to express someone's belief, and if so, how that expression fits with his experience? Why should he come up with it? Does he have some unusual perspective? We need, in short, to see how the role of this proposition has changed and to understand its new position. For it is no longer a truism. That change needs an explanation.

It is possible to understand the 'groundlessness' of the truisms in this light. They are groundless *because* they are truisms. One would like to say in addition: If they *were* used, they *would* express beliefs; but this is a dangerous inference. For the way we 'use' them in philosophy—as truisms—is inconsistent with their being beliefs and having supporting evidence. To imagine these propositions having ground or expressing beliefs is to imagine that they are propositions of a different sort altogether. It is to imagine them having a different status and a different role, and that would require different connections to the propositions which now entail them.

What does it mean to say there might have been evidence against the proposition that the world has existed many years and that it might have been false? It might mean that we can imagine a tribe of people for whom the proposition has a different role. In their language this proposition is not entailed by countless propositions expressing ordinary beliefs. On the contrary, this tribe believes that the world has existed only a short time, and they take various things as evidence that this is so.[27] For them, the proposition expresses a belief. But in saying this I do not think I have said enough to make clear *what* they would count as evidence, nor *how* they would discuss the truth of this proposition. We would need to know more about their other beliefs in order to understand. And this shows that the notion of 'evidence for a truism' is very queer. Inasmuch as something *is* a truism, 'evidence' for it is inapplicable, meaningless. But imagining it *not* to be a truism but to be belief-expressing still leaves utterly vague what evidence for it would be. How can we say one way or another without imagining a great deal more besides?[28]

It can be remarked here that a danger lies in a common philosophical use of the word 'presupposition.' A presupposition is often thought to be a proposition which, being entailed by the propositions that express our ordinary beliefs, expresses a belief fundamental to them.[29] So in finding such proposi-

27. Wittgenstein suggests this example: "Men have believed that they could make rain; why should not a king be brought up in the belief that the world began with him? And if Moore and this king were to meet and discuss, could Moore really prove his belief to be the right one?" (*On Certainty*, 92). The idea is not so unfamiliar: Plato provided such a myth for the first generation of his Republic.

28. There is a powerful temptation to say that we understand perfectly well what it would be for us *now* to believe that the world came into existence recently, or even five minutes ago. But understanding this surely means more than being familiar with English. A tribe whose members believed this would connect it with various things. To understand their belief we would need to understand how they regard ancient graveyards, etc., which would show what the belief means in that society.

29. Bradley, for one, seems to have meant this by 'presupposition' in his *Presuppositions of Critical History* (Chicago: Quadrangle, 1968), esp. pp. 83–96.

tions, one thinks to have found very important and basic beliefs, beliefs a thoroughly rational man might do well to question. But what we find is not beliefs but *propositions;* thus the question whether they are 'true' is not relevant. Nor does the demand that we find what they rest on have force or urgency any longer.

Propositions like the truisms and those about the reality of space and time and material things fascinate us. They do this because of their singular position with respect to other common, everyday sorts of propositions; this is to say, because of their extraordinary 'generality.' Our inclination is to treat them as superior and fundamental instances of contingent, belief-expressing propositions, and to ask the questions of them that we ask of the latter. But their location is crucial to understanding what sort of proposition they are. They stand, as Wittgenstein remarked, like an axis around which other things rotate; for in being entailed by such a number of belief-expressing propositions while not entailing others or themselves expressing beliefs, they each hold a position similar to the center of a circular design. But this location, it must be remembered, is that by which they were identified. We do not first find the truisms and then raise the question how they come to stand in such a central place. Their being truisms and their having this place are one. We identify them by means of a logical procedure *post hoc.* It should not be so difficult then to understand why they are not learned in childhood, at our parents' knees or in school; they have no use, and so 'learning' them makes no sense. We come to them rather by reflection, subsequent to learning and becoming thoroughly familiar with our language. And it is then we feel surprise that they have stood there, unnoticed, unexamined, and unsupported for so long! What we need to realize is precisely what we have found and where we have found it. What we have found in the truisms are not beliefs of a particularly fundamental sort. We have not found basic assumptions but grammatical artifacts. We did not find them by examining foundations but by digging in the cellar.

We can now better understand some of the curious features of Moore's argument. He should not have concerned himself *how* he knew the truisms, but also he should not have said *that he knew them.* 'I know' cannot with any clear meaning be fastened to such propositions. Wittgenstein was right that the result of doing this is very curious.[30] Yet they seem so indispensable, and no one certainly would deny them. They possess these features because of their connections with other propositions, not because they are themselves either certain or 'indispensable.' Indeed, that they are dispensable is shown by the fact that they are not attended to by nonphilosophers most of the time. They are 'indispensable' only in some grammatical sense and then only to philosophers. They do not behave like beliefs, as Wittgenstein remarked. They do not because, in short, they do not *express* beliefs. To consider their 'justification' is to treat them as something they simply are not.

It is appropriate to comment very briefly on the way Kant viewed such general propositions. He argued that propositions like 'Time is real' are not discoverable by experience, but their negations are not self-contradictory either. Therefore, they are like contingent propositions in some ways and like *a priori* ones in others. These characteristics made the propositions anomalies in a traditional classification of propositions; they are neither analytic nor contingent. To construe them in either way neglects features which belong to them and are important. Unlike the usual examples of contingent propositions, these do not express beliefs; unlike analytic propositions these derive from propositions which commonly *do* express beliefs. They do not have a use, but in some sense we would say that they have a 'meaning.' For they *derive* from propositions with meaning and do so in a straightforward way. It

---

30. Wittgenstein, *On Certainty*, 84.

would therefore be quite sensible to characterize them as synthetic and also as necessary.

A very original interpretation of the nature of Moore's truisms was given by Norman Malcolm.[31] He observed rightly that they are queer propositions for which we have no clear use, and that they don't express "common beliefs" or "things which we all commonly believe to be true."[32] Nevertheless they are important propositions and have great philosophical interest, and he views Moore's defense of them to be "a philosophical step of the first importance."[33]

The actual efficacy of Moore's reply, his misnamed "defence of common sense" consists in reminding us that there is a proper use for sentences like "I see the broom under the bed" or "It is known for certain that he drowned in the lake."[34]

It is such ordinary remarks as these which Moore really defends, according to Malcolm. The general propositions are not of themselves important, then. In the rightness of this purpose Malcolm concurs:

One is tempted to hold that certain ordinary expressions *cannot* have a correct use: at the same time one realizes that of course they *do*. Then one is in a muddle.[35]

Malcolm sees Moore's defense as a reminder to us that certain ways of speaking are quite correct despite philosophical arguments to the contrary. A philosopher should be watchful of conclusions which imply that such expressions are wrong, Malcolm argues; for they are *not* wrong, and from this the

31. I refer here to Malcolm's paper "George Edward Moore," in *Knowledge and Certainty*, rather than to his earlier essay, "Moore and Ordinary Language" (in the Schilpp volume on Moore), which contains a more radical 'linguistic' interpretation.

32. *Knowledge and Certainty*, pp. 168ff.

33. *Ibid.*, p. 182.

34. *Ibid.*, p. 181.

35. *Ibid.*, p. 183.

falsity of a philosophical view may directly follow. Malcolm thought that in calling philosophers back to the language of their everyday lives Moore was striking a powerful blow against skepticism.

It is difficult to fit Malcolm's interpretation with Moore's own remarks. Moore observed and was puzzled by the inconsistency of some philosophers as shown in their everyday habits versus their philosophical convictions. But he did not present this as a reminder; he used it to show that their philosophical views were wrong. He argued that, since it follows from certain philosophical views that great numbers of everyday beliefs are mistaken, the philosophical views cannot be right. Malcolm does not discuss the entailment of a philosophical generalization by everyday expressions of belief, but for Moore this is a central issue. Does such entailment constitute an argument? It is not clear that Moore always thinks it does; sometimes he speaks merely of the "loss of plausibility" of a view when its consequences are made evident. At other times he clearly means there is an argument to be made out. The everyday sentences Malcolm discusses are not problematic, but what does he make of the sentences 'Time is real,' 'Space is real'? If these are being used as 'reminders' by Moore, they nevertheless must have some other meaning besides, or he would not use them. In concentrating so on ordinary expressions of belief, Malcolm's defense weakens rather than strengthens Moore's argument.

This objection does not conflict with my judgment that Malcolm is right in emphasizing the importance of language and linguistic facts to this kind of dispute, for example, the dispute about the reality of time, space, and material things. The central question is what to make of the entailment by ordinary propositions of such extraordinary ones.

I turn now to find illumination by considering the arguments of Bradley and McTaggart to show that time is *not* real. For it is not yet clear what the propositions 'Time is real'

and 'Space is real' are meant to deny, nor is it clear what can
be meant by denying them.

3

How should a dispute come about whether time is real?
The sentence 'Time is real' has no ordinary use the way 'Time
flies' and 'The danger is real' do. While its components are
everyday, the whole is not. The sentence does not express a
belief; it does not even occur outside philosophy. And there,
moreover, its meaning can be seen to be altogether derivative.
It can be accounted for only in terms of the meaningful sentences from which it is derived. Furthermore, its negation,
'Time is unreal' is more curious still. One is inclined to say
offhand both that it is false and that it is meaningless. It cries
for an explanation. To understand the dispute about the reality of time we therefore need to look at some arguments for
saying that time is not real. In this way we shall understand
somewhat better what it was Moore wanted to refute.

McTaggart gave this argument for the unreality of time:
Essential to the concept of time are the distinctions 'past,'
'present,' 'future.' It is essential to time that moments in time
form a series (McTaggart calls it the "A series") in which
some moments are past, some are present, and some future.
The predicates 'past,' 'present,' and 'future' are incompatible,
of course. Yet, McTaggart says, moments have all three; and
here is a contradiction. In the face of this contradiction, we
must conclude that the A series cannot exist; but without it
there is no such thing as time. Time is therefore unreal.[36]

To an obvious objection McTaggart offers a simple defense:

[It will be objected:] The characteristics are only incompatible
when they are simultaneous, and there is no contradiction to this
in the fact that each term has all of them successively.

36. "The Unreality of Time," in J. McTaggart, *Philosophical
Studies* (New York: Books for Libraries Press, 1968), pp. 111ff. I have
simplified McTaggart's argument somewhat here.

But this explanation involves a vicious circle. For it assumes the existence of time in order to account for the way in which moments are past, present, and future. Time then must be presupposed to account for the A series. But we have already seen that the A series has to be assumed in order to account for time.[37]

What is the conclusion to be drawn? McTaggart answers:

We have come then to the conclusion that the application of the A series to reality involves a contradiction, and that consequently the A series cannot be true of reality. . . . Whenever we judge anything to exist in time, we are in error. And whenever we perceive anything as existing in time—which is the only way in which we ever do perceive things—we are perceiving it more or less as it really is not.[38]

McTaggart is not in disagreement with Moore about the consequences of denying that time is real. It does conflict with things we ordinarily assert and entails that they are false. Whenever we judge things to be happening over a certain time or say one thing happens before another or that two events are simultaneous, we are mistaken. I call attention to this because it shows that McTaggart for one did not need to be 'reminded' that his contention conflicts with ordinary remarks. It would not have been an original feature of Moore's argument, then, to point this out.

The question is, how could McTaggart reconcile himself to rejecting as false all those everyday remarks? How could he be reconciled to their falsity while he himself continued to speak of being ready for dinner at seven or having walked for a half an hour or getting to his lectures on time? Why didn't he take the course Moore and Malcolm suggest, of inferring that there must be something wrong with his argument? McTaggart addressed the issue of these difficult consequences. He explained that we get our idea of time from

37. *Ibid.*, p. 124.
38. *Ibid.*, p. 126,

perception together with the idea that perception takes place in the present, while memory and anticipation look to the past and future.[39] This is how we arrive at the notion of the A series of moments. However, we are deceived about the character of perception; there is no real present for it to be lodged in. Rather the present is not clearly distinguishable from the past and future. Therefore the A series does not correspond to anything in reality.

And so it would seem that the denial of the reality of time is not so very paradoxical after all. It was called paradoxical because it seemed to contradict our experience so violently—to compel us to treat so much as illusion which appears *prima facie* to give knowledge of reality. But we now see that our experience of time—centring as it does about the specious present—would be no less illusory if there were a real time in which the realities we experience existed. The specious present of our observations—varying as it does from you to me—cannot correspond to the present of events observed. . . . On either hypothesis—whether we take time as real or as unreal—everything is observed in a specious present, but nothing, not even the observations themselves, can ever *be* in a specious present. And in that case I do not see that we treat experience as much more illusory when we say that nothing is ever in a present at all, than when we say that everything passes through some entirely different present.[40]

The entire paradoxical situation seems to revolve around the specious present and the relativity of perception to an observer. McTaggart thinks that saying time is real goes against common sense as much as saying time is unreal. There is no solution compatible with the common-sense view.

McTaggart was neither neglectful of the implications of his view for common sense nor altogether comfortable with them. Perception—or what we usually think of as perception—requires conditions that cannot be. As a result, what we mean by time cannot correspond to anything in reality. This does

39. *Ibid.*, pp. 129–130.
40. *Ibid.*

not dictate that we should no longer speak as we are used to. What alternative would there be to that anyway? But we cannot suppose that the things we speak of in everyday exchange are necessarily real. One does not get the impression here that McTaggart is either disdainful of common-sense beliefs or in combat against them. Rather he seems to accept what is logically inevitable.

C. A. Campbell once remarked that a philosophical skeptic can make his own appeal to the common man:

> If anyone should feel the need of a proof that the plain man really understands that "knowing for certain" means "knowing in a way that excludes the possibility of doubt," I don't think he will need to search far to obtain it. Let him show the plain man hitherto unsuspected grounds for doubt in the case of any proposition at all which the plain man has been in the habit of thinking, and saying, he "knew for certain". If the plain man appreciates these grounds, he will at once confess that he does not, after all, know for certain.[41]

Campbell remarks that teachers of philosophy have plenty of experience observing students as their convictions change from 'common sense' ones to those of skepticism. And we have seen that a number of skeptical arguments have a very simple form, appealing directly to a nonphilosopher. A student might then find McTaggart's argument compelling and Moore's response excessively blunt.

The issue here is whether and how a conflict with common sense should count as a criticism of a philosophical view. It seems now even more necessary to consider the *kinds* of argument on each side. On his side, Moore follows what is entailed by ordinary everyday remarks about time, to the conclusion that time is real. He does not attack McTaggart's premises.[42]

41. "Common Sense Propositions and Philosophical Paradoxes," *Proceedings of the Aristotelian Society*, 45 (1944/45), 9.
42. Moore does attack some of McTaggart's and Bradley's premises elsewhere, e.g., in *SMPP*, Chs. 10–12; and in *Lectures in Philosophy*, Lecture III.

On the other side, McTaggart is following out implications he finds contained in the ordinary and everyday concept of time. This concept requires impossible conditions; therefore it cannot represent or signify something real. Both arguments begin with common speech and everyday remarks. How can one choose between them?

Before exploring this question, I turn to an argument of F. H. Bradley's that time is not real but apparent. Bradley argues that, on the one hand, we conceive of time as a stream which is continuous but composed of temporal units. On the other hand, we speak of it as a relation between moments, moments without duration. Now both of these conceptions lead to difficulty.

If you take time as a relation between units without duration, then the whole time has no duration, and is not time at all. But if you give duration to the whole time, then at once the units themselves are found to possess it; and they thus cease to be units. Time in fact is 'before' and 'after' in one; and without this diversity it is not time. But these differences cannot be asserted of the unity; and . . . time is helplessly dissolved.[43]

Our concept of time is fraught with paradoxes, many of them. Therefore time cannot be real any more than anything else whose concept is self-contradictory. If time is thought of as a relation between durationless moments, then there is no ground for duration. But if it is thought of as continuous duration, it will lack temporal units and there cannot be discriminations within it. We speak about time in a variety of ways, under various metaphors. And one way of speaking conflicts with another; time cannot be what we presume it must. What must follow if this were so? Time and space,

43. *Appearance and Reality* (Oxford: Oxford University Press, 51), pp. 33–34. I avoid discussing what Bradley took the denial of 'Time is real' to mean, which would involve a discussion of his complicated doctrine of 'Appearance.'

Bradley says, are concepts "vitiated by self-discrepancy."[44] They cannot therefore belong to Reality.

Bradley explains his way of arguing about what is and is not real:

> Is there an absolute criterion of [what is real?] . . . How otherwise should we be able to say anything at all about appearance? . . . We were judging phenomena and were condemning them, and throughout proceeded as if the self-contradictory could not be real. But this was surely to have and to apply an absolute criterion. . . . Ultimate reality is such that it does not contradict itself; here is an absolute criterion.[45]

Nothing self-contradictory can be real. And so much is self-contradictory Bradley feels no need to distinguish between a criterion and a *sine qua non*. Could anyone, could Moore, object to this? Moore agreed that self-contradiction would show that something was not so, was not real. But he did not use it as a criterion, for he had a different one. He viewed the matter this way:

> It seems to me I have an absolutely conclusive argument to show that none of [the truisms] does entail both of two incompatible propositions. Namely this: All of [those] propositions . . . are true; no true proposition entails both of two incompatible propositions; therefore, none of [these] propositions . . . entails both of two incompatible propositions.[46]

Moore appears almost to be mocking Bradley here. For his remarks heighten the paradoxical situation of their disagreement. He calls attention to the fact that they *agree* that what describes reality must be consistent; but they disagree about where to begin the description of what is real. Moore would substitute for Bradley's criterion the criterion: what is true of reality is what follows from what I certainly know. But the

44. *Ibid.*, p. 119.
45. *Ibid.*, p. 120.
46. 'DCS', p. 41.

fact that Moore's method is not Bradley's does not dispel the mystery what to make of the radical differences in their conclusions.

What would Moore say, one wonders, if he were faced with a contradiction as McTaggart and Bradley were? We are mistaken if we think Moore always argued from common-sense premises which he knew to be true. Consider the following argument without such premises, where Moore invokes the concepts of 'self-evidence' and 'contradiction' in connection with a classical metaphysical problem. The issue is time's infinity.

> This assumption [that time is infinite] merely involves the principles that *before* any or every length of time, there must be *one* other equal to it, and that *after* any or every length of time, there must be *one* other equal to it, and therefore an infinite number. What are we to say of these two principles? They do seem to me to be self-evident; but I confess I do not know exactly how to set about arguing that they are self-evident. The chief thing to be done is, I think, to consider them as carefully and distinctly as possible and then to see whether it does not seem as if they *must* be true; and to compare them with other propositions, which do seem to be certainly true, and then to consider whether you have any better reason for supposing these other propositions to be true than for supposing this one to be so.[47]

The two principles about time are self-evident, but how can one *argue* that they are? Moore provides us with a technique: compare such a principle with something you are utterly certain about, and observe whether the latter is more certain than the former. What kind of proposition are we to take to make the test?

Consider, for instance, the proposition that since I began to lecture this evening, *some* time certainly has elapsed. Have you any better reason for believing this, than for believing that, if so, a

47. *SMPP*, p. 191; italics are Moore's.

length of time equal to this one must have elapsed *before* it? And that this must be true of every length of time equal to that which has elapsed since I began to lecture? I cannot see that you have any better reason for believing the one proposition than for believing the other.[48]

Moore puts weight again on what is known in a mundane ordinary way, but the role of such knowledge here is curious. We are asked to compare two propositions and to ask ourselves whether they are of equal certainty. It appears to be a sort of *Gedankenexperiment*. And yet it isn't clear how we make the test. How can Moore suppose we will all agree about the result? I think that something analogous to our ear for music is involved here; but what we need to discriminate is not sound but certainty. For Moore's experiment to be a test, we have to imagine something like this: we say each proposition to ourselves, and while doing this observe our own attitude toward each—toward the certainty of each. In this process we are depending on our ability to judge and compare certainties. We are discriminating between more and less certainty, not by giving reasons but by observation.

Using this method, Moore determines that the principles showing time to be infinite are self-evident, and he concludes that the notion of infinite time has "no obscurity or inconceivability or lack of clearness or distinctness."[49] Yet as Moore proceeds he discovers difficulties in the general notion of an infinite series. He finds himself led into contradiction and paradox. At that point he asks, "Does it follow that it is impossible that there should be such an infinite series?"[50] He is, at this juncture, precisely at the point where Bradley and McTaggart found themselves when they followed the implications contained in the notion of time. How can Moore an-

48. *Ibid.*, pp. 191–192; Moore's italics.
49. *Ibid.*
50. *Ibid.*, p. 198.

swer this? His answer is illuminating for his dispute with the idealists:

For my part, I do not know exactly what conclusion ought to be drawn from all these arguments. They are, I think, an excellent example of the way in which philosophical arguments can make things seem uncertain which, at first, seemed very certain. But it does seem to me that we certainly are not entitled to draw the positive conclusion, which some philosophers have drawn, to the effect that there are no such things as inches, feet, yards and miles, or as seconds, minutes, hours, and years.[51]

He will not concede that time and space are unreal. But neither does he have an answer to the contradictions. His observation that this is the sort of argument which unsettles one about the most obvious things is right; the question is what is one to make of such arguments? Moore does not provide us with an answer.

Moore's arguments began from premises that are part of our ordinary ways of expressing beliefs. The truisms, that is, were rooted in speech of a common sort. From these also flowed the propositions that time and space and material things are real. And from these too flowed the propositions that time and space are infinite. Yet eventually these led to contradiction. Bradley's and McTaggart's arguments began with general remarks about time and space. Yet these premises, like the truisms, originate in ordinary talk about time and space. That time is measurable durations seems obvious to anyone who speaks English; that it is a series of moments is equally apparent. That it is infinite and infinitely divisible would also be granted by anyone interested in reflecting upon it. These are the kinds of general remarks which led to contradictions. Although Moore's method led to the conclusion that time is real and Bradley's and McTaggart's to the conclusion that time is unreal, the ultimate origins of both arguments

51. *Ibid.*, p. 200; Moore's italics.

are similar. And one can argue that, inasmuch as both sides uncovered contradictions regarding time, the focus of the dispute *should* be what to make of contradictions discovered in either of these ways.

Consider the proposition 'Time is real.' It seems, as Moore claimed, to follow from unquestionable truths about the world and events. And the same is true of the reality of space. Yet from asserting that time and space are real, contradictions seem derivable. And that is for Bradley a signal to stop:

> We either do not know what space means; and, if so, certainly we cannot say that it is more than appearance. Or else, knowing what we mean by it, we see inherent in that meaning the puzzle we are describing. Space, to be space, must have space outside itself.[52]

We cannot accept a concept which has contradictory consequences. Yet the contradictions of space and time are old subjects in philosophy.[53] Kant showed us in his antinomies how we derived such contradictions and what was the matter with such reasoning.[54] But the contradictions are unresolved still and the strict validity of the arguments has gone largely unchallenged. Musn't we wonder what to make of this situation and what, in particular, a common-sense conclusion can be grounded in?

Even Hume showed respect for the contradictions connected with space and time:

> The chief objection against all *abstract* reasonings is derived from the ideas of space and time; ideas, which in common life and to a careless view, are very clear and intelligible, but when they pass through the scrutiny of the profound sciences . . . afford prin-

52. Bradley, *Appearance and Reality*, p. 32.

53. Aristotle called attention to some paradoxical features of time in *Physics*, Bk. IV, Chs. 10–11. He was determined to resolve them, however, so that 'time' should be a consistent idea.

54. *Critique of Pure Reason* N. K. Smith, trans. (New York: St. Martins, 1965), Second Division, Book II, Ch. II, pp. 396–398,

ciples which seem full of absurdity and contradiction. No priestly *dogmas*, invented on purpose to tame and subdue the rebellious reason of mankind, ever shocked common sense more than the doctrine of the infinitive divisibility of extension, with its consequences. . . . But what renders the matter more extraordinary, is, that these seemingly absurd opinions are supported by a chain of reasoning, the clearest and most natural; nor is it possible for us to allow the premise without admitting the consequences.[55]

Common sense is shocked, yet no flaw is apparent in the inference. What better characterization could be given of the dispute between Moore and the idealists? Faced with these contradictions, reason suffers, Hume continues, and "seems thrown into a kind of amazement and suspence, which, without the suggestions of any sceptic, gives her a diffidence of herself, and of the ground on which she treads."[56] And Reason being so corrupted, only skepticism can benefit:

Yet still reason must remain restless, and unquiet, even with regard to that scepticism, to which she is driven by these seeming absurdities and contradictions. How any clear, distinct idea can contain circumstances contradictory to itself, or to any other clear, distinct idea, is absolutely incomprehensible; and is, perhaps, as absurd as any proposition which can be formed.[57]

Here Hume, like Moore, tends to give pre-eminence to common sense over the demands of logic. What could be more absurd than such a clear notion as 'time' being contradictory! Like Moore he seems to say he is so certain of this common notion as to be sure nothing contradictory *can* follow from it! Yet Hume's "restless reason" compelled him to suggest in a footnote that perhaps the issue might be resolved by supposing that ideas of quantity are not general but particular, a most unnatural supposition.[58] And so the issue: which should take

55. *An Enquiry Concerning Human Understanding*, p. 156.
56. *Ibid.*, p. 157.
57. *Ibid.*, pp. 157–158.
58. *Ibid.*, n, p. 158. Hume does not give the impression he is satisfied

precedence, rational argument or common sense? swung him first toward the one answer and then toward the other.

This is our predicament: In pursuing the consequences which seem clearly to flow from our ordinary talk about time, we run straight into contradictions, not just one but several. The same is true of deriving consequences from our concept of space. As Hume says, there are not complicated or doubtful steps in the inferences: on the one hand, time must be infinite, but if it is infinite, it loses its claim to be a defined whole or unity. It must be durational; but if so, it cannot be composed of nondurational parts or moments. And so on. These contradictory notions are all rooted in ordinary language. What force can 'common sense' exert, therefore, in opposing them? That line of defense appears closed.

But if we have no defense against the contradictions and no rightful criticism of their source, perhaps we should look further at the significance of contradiction. Perhaps we should ask what follows when such a contradiction is found. *Must* we conclude, with Bradley, that time is unreal and only apparent? Or if not, must we, with Moore and Hume, deny that any contradiction is there, at the risk of conceding that if they are, then 'time' and 'space' are meaningless? The alternatives are harsh. Let us look more carefully at what has been proved.

Let us concede that contradictions follow from the concepts of time and space, as Kant, Bradley, Hume, McTaggart and even Moore maintained.[59] We concede then that there

---

with this answer. He writes: "It certainly concerns all lovers of science not to expose themselves to the ridicule and contempt of the ignorant by their conclusions; and this seems the readiest solution of their difficulties" (*ibid.*).

59. I do not want to claim that all the 'contradictions' here are irresoluble. No doubt some are instances of error, e.g., the treatment of a duration or a line as a collection of points. But part of the argument for such a claim would be that the concept of time cannot be contradictory; and this is the proposition needing elucidation.

are contradictory propositions about time, both of which can be 'proved' by reference to ordinary ways of talking of time and conceiving of it. Compare the situation to that of light in modern physical theory: in certain kinds of problems light is treated as molecular; in other problems it is treated as a wave. These two ways of treating it are distinct, yet they both connect with phenomena of light and are not unrelated. Why should we not be concerned with this 'contradiction'? Why should we not say that the physicists contradict themselves in speaking of light in these two different ways? The answer a physicist would give is that it is not a matter of the light *being* a particle in the one context and its *being* a wave in the other. The formulas in which light is involved do not represent his beliefs about what light *is*. Therefore, though it is no doubt unfortunate that his theory is disjointed in some respects, he would maintain there is no real contradiction.

What sort of defense does this represent? It charges that the issue is not one of contradictory *beliefs*, and therefore the contradictory propositions are harmless. Such a defense is instructive for philosophy. In Chapter IV I argued that contradictions are problematic only when two conflicting beliefs are involved; contradictions that are mere propositions, expressing *no* belief, are not in a serious sense contradictory. But is not this last the case with the contradictions concerning time? Does the proposition that time is infinite, for instance, express a belief? Does the proposition that time is composed of nondurational moments do so? Or the proposition that time is infinitely divisible? What sort of situation might there be—outside philosophical discussions—in which such a belief might be expressed? One can hardly imagine any. This situation is parallel to that of the physicist; he does not, for example, attempt to persuade someone else that light *is, as he believes,* a wave and not a particle. It is not an issue which needs to be decided either way. Why not—are these two propositions not intrinsically incompatible? That is the question. If you say they are incompatible *as propositions*, that must be understood not to imply that they express incompatible beliefs. For they do not. They are not incompatible in the sense that you cannot live with both. Each has its role to play in calculations concerned with light, and both are needed. Their 'inconsistency' would become a problem only if each expressed a belief and those beliefs were incompatible.[60]

That time is durational is a proposition derived in a respectable way, and other propositions about time conflicting with it are equally defensible. But the fact that these propositions derive from other propositions which express beliefs does not justify the claim that *they* represent beliefs. And there is no justification of any other kind for saying that they do. What we have derived is propositions of an interesting sort.[61] It is only unclear what their role is. Consider in this respect the two principle claims in dispute: Time is real; Time is unreal. What, if we are deciding between them, would we be deciding *about*? I mean what is it to hold that time *is* real as opposed to holding that it *isn't*? I don't know what it would be, unless it is to prefer one set of arguments to another. But this choice is nowise necessary. We can accept both sets of argument and do so without uneasiness or throwing our reason

60. Other examples of philosophical paradoxes which have roots firmly stuck in ordinary discourse are Parmenides's paradox of 'nonbeing' and the 'liar' paradox. Bradley was right in saying there are contradictions everywhere. But this shows us something about 'contradiction,' not about what may be 'real.'

61. Aristotle, in defending the law of contradiction, argues: "And can he be wrong who believes something is either so or not so, and he be right who believes both? If the latter is right, what could he mean by making such a statement about the nature of things?" Aristotle repeatedly argues that one cannot believe contradictions, showing that this notion is fundamentally connected with belief and not a relation between propositions (*Metaphysics*, R. Hope, trans. [Ann Arbor: University of Michigan Press, 1968], p. 75); other similar passages can be found throughout Book Gamma.

into amazement and suspense. For in accepting both propositions and the arguments for them we do not commit ourselves
to beliefs.

This conclusion goes against much that is assumed in the
practice of giving philosophical arguments. Are we not dedi-
cated to making rational what is given to us in an incoherent
and jumbled form? Is it not our business to follow out the
consequences of our beliefs to see what is involved? And
when we come upon a contradiction, are we not right to call
a halt and concern ourselves with its source? How else can
reason, as Hume would say, enter combat against superstition
and prejudice?

My argument has shown that certain kinds of philosophical
inferences have no concern with our beliefs. They may
originate with belief and its ordinary expressions. But they
soon concern propositions merely and there is no connection
between these propositions and our actual, functioning language except the derivation which led to them. I argue that
we do not need to—and indeed should not—construe these
propositions as belief-expressing. They are not; no account of
them shows they have an ordinary belief-expressing use.

But now it is a serious question what we are doing when we
make such philosophical inferences. What is the point of these
propositions? What purpose is served by discovering them?
One can give an answer but it is an answer that will not satisfy
many philosophers: What we find is propositions which the
grammar of ordinary expressions seems to point to. We find
propositions which represent, almost like schemata, the grammar of certain expressions in our language. To say that time is
duration is to say that our language concerning time takes a
certain cast—a certain form—of expression. But to say time is
composed of moments means that talk about time takes *that*
form or grammar. How can it take both? It just does. The
way we refer to time varies with different contexts, just as the
way what we call an 'animal' and what a 'plant' varies, just as

whether we treat light as a wave or particle varies, just as whether we use feet or centimeters varies. None of these different ways of speaking of one thing indicate a difference in beliefs. Beliefs are not involved; only forms of speaking. One can think of such a proposition as the imaginary center of a design, made of ordinary ways of speaking. The rest of the design entails it and in a sense requires it; yet the proposition itself has no role or function. Or you might say, its function is just to be so entailed and required.

What I have said about contradictions is reminiscent of and connected with Wittgenstein's remarks about contradiction in mathematics. When faced with a queer and contradictory sentence, he suggests saying:

That is what comes of making up such sentences. —But there is a contradiction here! Well, then there is a contradiction here. Does it do any harm here?[62]

I have argued that contradictions found in philosophy do not do any 'harm' so long as the propositions do not express beliefs, and most of them do not. (It is not clear what the comparable proviso would be for mathematical contradictions, or whether there is one.) Of the generation of such unusable propositions in philosophy Wittgenstein wrote:

Is there harm in the contradiction that arises when someone says: "I am lying,—So I am not lying. —So I am lying.—etc?" I mean: does it make our language less usable if in this case, according to the ordinary rules, a proposition yields its contradictory, and vice versa?—. . . . The proposition *itself* is unusable, and these inferences equally; but why should they not be made? —It is a profitless performance![63]

I do not concede that it is 'profitless' to make philosophical inferences even though they lead to unusable propositions or

62. *Remarks on the Foundations of Mathematics*, Part I, Appendix I, 11.
63. *Ibid.*, 12.

to paradoxical ones. There *is* a kind of illumination gained, for the subject of the propositions is our concepts, and their properties are put more or less clearly before us. Nevertheless these inferences have some similarities to moves in a game. The inferences we make do not lead to beliefs, nor do they lead to any functional result. We follow them in the spirit of tracing a design—a grammatical one—to its completion.[64] And should we not wonder where it will lead—how the completed shape will appear? The concepts are our own, and our interest in their shapes and connections is natural. It is a game that intrigues us.

4

Moore's defense of common sense takes on a different look in the light of this conclusion. Moore was 'defending' things that seemed to him true and obvious, and defending them on the grounds that they accorded with common sense, as the propositions of Bradley and McTaggart did not. Of course the proposition 'Time is unreal' has an absurd sound, dissonant and wrong. It *sounds* metaphysical, while 'Time is real' sounds more sensible. But then Bradley enjoyed asserting things that were surprising and paradoxical while Moore did not. Moore preferred to assert what was—even obviously—true and right in contradiction to those who asserted what was paradoxical and strange. In this way he was a 'common sense philosopher.' He held to what sounded right even so far as to grant that an implied contradiction might just have to stand unrefuted; perhaps his distrust of philosophical reasoning led him this far. However, Moore failed to see the real nature of his dispute with the idealists. Neither of the propositions 'Time is real' or 'Time is unreal' expressed beliefs, not common-sense

64. Wittgenstein once compared mathematical equations to ornaments or wallpaper patterns. This image is appropriate here (*ibid.*, Part V, 33).

beliefs or any other kind. But if they did not express beliefs, what was there to defend? Only propositions. And a proposition is not something appropriately 'defended.'

Malcolm's interpretation came close to the truth, for he claimed that normal *ways of speaking* were being defended, not *beliefs*, expressed by such truisms as Moore's. Malcolm realized the error of calling these beliefs. Yet he stops short of the inference that the dispute is one over propositions merely, that the two sides were far more similar in their arguments than either thought, and that, finally, they could coexist.

I wish to return again to the question what sort of inference G. E. Moore on his side and the idealists on theirs make from our ordinary expressions of belief. For, as we have seen, they are 'inferences' in a rather extraordinary and philosophical sense. In view of the fact that they so easily lead to contradictory propositions, we might well ask what justifies us in making them.

How can we justify the inference from ordinary propositions about events to the reality of time? If we were asked to justify some everyday inference, for example, from the sound of the whistle to the existence of a fire nearby, we would cite some circumstance connecting the two things. But the case of entailments is plainly different. We do not cite connections; the connection is presumably there in the sentences themselves. From the fact that something is iron, it follows that it is metal, and does so because iron is a metal. No 'circumstance' should or can come between and connect them. We recognize the entailment as a part of knowing the meanings of 'iron' and 'metal.' This then must be the case with the connection between ordinary propositions and the proposition that time is real. From the proposition that I took a walk before lunch follows the proposition that some things happen before others; and from this proposition follows the proposition that time is real. But something rather strange happens in these two steps. I want to say that the proposition that some things happen

before others has a fairly clear sense. It does not seem problematic. On the other hand I do not know what 'Time is real'
means. It is certainly not *clear* what it means. How therefore
should I feel comfortable with inferring it from the other,
which is fairly clear? This situation is not unlike inferences
made in mathematics regarding infinity. I can understand the
infinity of natural numbers; but I don't feel that I clearly
understand 'comparing' infinities and having various infinite
numbers. The inferences go beyond my grasp. I can see and
understand how they originate, but that does not assure me
that they end in something I also understand.

We are often in philosophy inclined to trust our ear for
inferences about very abstract matters. Thus, it sounds all
right to infer that time is real from the fact that some things
happen before others. After all, time could not be *un*real could
it? But this kind of inference-by-ear is hazardous. Consider the
following inference of Moore's. He offers as an explanation
of the proposition that time is infinite "that before any or
every length of time, there must have elapsed one other equal
to it, and that after any or every length of time there must be
one equal to it."[65] Now we do understand perfectly well the
expressions, 'a long time,' 'some length of time,' 'an equally
long time'—expressions that *appear* to explain all the content
of Moore's explanatory proposition. But although these everyday expressions are clear and their use unambiguous, it is a different case with 'every length of time' and 'any length of time.'
What can one make of the expression 'every length of time'?
How many are there in an hour, say? Obviously the question
doesn't make sense. How can lengths be distinguished? If they
cannot, then how can the set of *all* of them be defined? I for
one have no idea. I do not understand 'a length of time' when
it is used in this general way. It is not like 'a piece of 8½ × 11
paper,' which refers to an identifiable and collectable unit.

65. *SMPP*, p. 191.

Nor am I sure what it means for a length of time to 'exist,' nor therefore what it means to say there 'must be' some. These expressions are empty, blank. Perhaps their meaning is metaphorical; then what are they metaphors *of*?

I am calling attention, in this example, to the danger of inferring from expressions which have a particular everyday use to generalizations which have none. The situation here is similar to that with 'all that one knows.' We have an everyday use for the expression, but that is not a good ground for inferring there is a set of all the things we know. Such a set would be an anomaly within a description of what 'knowing' means. Wittgenstein remarked that we have a "craving for generality"; perhaps it is satisfied by making inferences from particular and everyday assertions to abstract and general ones. But in making the inferences, we sometimes—as does Moore in the instance above—forfeit meaning.

The general source of such inferences is the supposition that whatever we infer from a proposition which is meaningful and expresses belief, will also be meaningful and belief-expressing. But neither meaningfulness nor truth can be made to rest on this ground. The meanings of everyday expressions do not tell us how to interpret general assertions, for example, about durations, infinite extent, infinite divisibility, and sheer momentariness. The general propositions about these do not wait to be uncovered at the foundations of our beliefs. They stand at the outer limits of a chain of inferences, each step less firm than the one preceding it. At each step the derived meanings become more ghostly.

General propositions about time and space can, I suggest, be thought of as representations of grammatical patterns, patterns that are familiar but unremarked in our usual employment of the expressions. Viewed in this way, it is very curious to call such propositions 'true.' And viewed in this way we do not need to see the 'contradictions' of Bradley and McTaggart and Moore as instances of conflict. Either of two 'contradictory' patterns can be traced; it depends on where we start. Understood in this way, they clearly do not present us with a 'view of the world' (and then of course not a contradictory one); no more are the truisms part of a 'common sense' view. They do not express or embody views. They are curious and interesting representations of grammar.[66]

66. After completing this chapter, I became acquainted with Alice Ambrose's discussion of the dispute between Moore and the idealists ("Commanding a Clear View of Philosophy," Presidential Address, American Philosophical Association Meetings, New York, 1975). That discussion, like mine, takes this dispute over time and space as a paradigm which can illuminate the nature of philosophy and philosophical method. Professor Ambrose provided me with some helpful comments on this subject.

VII

Dead Certainty

Is anything entirely certain? Is there, as Bertrand Russell once asked, "any knowledge in the world which is so certain that no reasonable man could doubt it."[1] Surely this is one of the first questions to ask concerning knowledge. And the possible answers to it are clear-cut: either something is certain and provable or nothing is.

Though natural and compelling, the question lays the ground for skepticism. One may, like Descartes, be "constrained to confess that there is nothing in all that I formerly believed to be true of which I cannot in some measure doubt, and that . . . for reasons which are very powerful and maturely considered."[2] Yet we ask of ordinary matters whether they are certain: the general question, What is certain? lies only one step beyond these ordinary ones. How puzzling that such a plain question should lead directly to skepticism—to the

1. *The Problems of Philosophy*, p. 7.
2. *Philosophical Works*, I, 145.

view that nothing whatever is known! In the present chapter I consider how this comes about.

1

What is desired is absolute certainty. But what is the force here of 'absolute?' The answer is: Whatever is not absolutely certain is therefore in some degree doubtful. Absolute certainty means certainty of the very highest degree, certainty without the least hint of hesitation or doubt. When we say, for example, that something is practically certain or nearly certain we make room for being mistaken. We speak without the maximum assurance. Our remark is thus compared with that stronger statement we might have made, one showing utter and unqualified certainty. This latter, then, is the kind of certainty we want when we ask whether anything is known.

It is common to say that something is almost certain or practically certain, to say that one thing is less certain than another, that it is equally certain, half as certain or twice as certain as another. Sometimes these are judgments of probability, resting on evidence which allows us to compare and measure one likelihood with another. But just as often probabilities are not involved. We can ask how certain this matter is, and how certain in comparison with that one, without implying that measures exist by which an answer can be determined. How can we make such judgments as these?[3]

The question is similar to the question, How do we determine whether we know or only believe a certain thing? In Chapter II I argued that such questions arise only in certain situations, and their answers express attitudes or give assurance relative to those situations. They do not reveal ongoing

3. Moore as well as Descartes speaks of comparing propositions to see which is the more certain. See e.g., Section 3, Chapter VI, above, in particular the passages cited in n. 51.

attitudes standing apart from the context in which the question arose. Is the case similar with respect to the question what, if anything, is known? Here we seem to ask of the things we believe whether they are certain, whether any of them are. The question doesn't apparently concern us or our situation but rather the things themselves. We ask: are *they* certain?

Asking what is certain suggests that the things we believe can be graded according to their certainty, as apples in a basket can be graded according to firmness or color. Only those of the utmost certainty—those which are in Descartes's words "entirely certain and indubitable"—are of interest.[4] The question depends therefore on the assumption that there is a class of all the things we believe, a class of objects of belief. Chapter V showed that there is no justification for speaking of such a class, any more than there is for speaking of a class of things we know. Therefore the sorting of what is absolutely certain cannot be, as we first think, the sorting of things in a given collection.

Nevertheless we can and do discriminate things as more or less certain, we can and do compare their degrees of certainty with no reference to probabilities, and the question is what is meant by doing this? How do we do it, and what does it imply for the question what, if anything, is certain?

One account of such a distinction was put forward by Norman Malcolm in the form of a distinction between 'strong' and 'weak' senses of 'know.' According to Malcolm, knowing in the strong sense corresponds to what philosophers have usually meant by "perfect" or "metaphysical" or "strict" certainty.[5] His account can therefore be taken then as both an explanation of absolute certainty and a defense that such certainty exists.

Malcolm characterized the difference between strong and weak knowing in the following way:

4. *Philosophical Works*, I, 148.
5. *Knowledge and Certainty*, p. 70.

When I use "know" in the weak sense I am prepared to let an investigation (demonstration, calculation) determine whether the something that I claim to know is true or false. When I use "know" in the strong sense I am not prepared to look upon anything as an *investigation;* I do not concede that anything whatever could prove me mistaken; I do not regard the matter as open to any *question.*[6]

The attitude characterized as 'knowing in the strong sense' is one we take on "innumerable occasions of daily life" toward various statements, according to Malcolm.[7] We have this attitude toward $2 + 2 = 4$, for instance, and towards some non-mathematical statements as well. In contrast there are many things we know of which we are not so certain, regarding which a proof would be interesting and might serve to persuade or dissuade us. For Malcolm such a statement is 'There is a heart in my body.' His belief about this might be shaken.[8] His attitude toward it is not perfectly secure or fixed. The two attitudes he distinguishes in this way Malcolm says are part of the logical character of the statements. For how we regard the statements determines their relations to the concepts of confirmation and disproof.

Malcolm seems to imply that we have these attitudes toward statements that are actually made. But when, one may ask, do we have occasion to assert that $2 + 2 = 4$? When do we ever say we know it? And if we never do, then do we nevertheless have the attitude which *would be* expressed if we *did* say we knew it? Malcolm recognizes the importance of providing a use for the proposition that we know that $2 + 2 = 4$ and he describes one:

It is hard to think of circumstances in which it would be natural for me to say that I know that $2 + 2 = 4$ because no one ever

6. *Ibid.,* p. 64; Malcolm's italics.
7. *Ibid.,* pp. 68–69.
8. *Ibid.,* p. 66.

questions it. Let us try to suppose, however, that someone whose intelligence I respect argues that certain developments in arithmetic have shown that 2 + 2 does not equal 4. He writes out a proof of this in which I can find no flaw. Suppose that his demeanor showed me that he was in earnest. Suppose that several persons of normal intelligence become persuaded that his proof was correct and that 2 + 2 does not equal 4. What would be my reaction? I should say "I can't see what is wrong with your proof; but it *is* wrong, because I *know* that 2 + 2 = 4." Here I should be using "know" in its strong sense. I should not admit that my argument or any future development in mathematics could show that it is false that 2 + 2 = 4.[9]

Malcolm's assertion that he knows that 2 + 2 = 4 involves the strong sense of 'know' and expresses his attitude of firm conviction. However, there is a difficulty here, remarked in Chapter II: the 'attitude' expressed by saying he knows cannot be an attitude toward the statement "2 + 2 = 4," for no such statement was made. Nor does it seem reasonable to think that 'know' generally must refer to a statement which someone has actually made. What Malcolm's account seems to require is the term 'proposition.' But then it is vulnerable to the criticisms given earlier against calling propositions the objects of knowledge.

But there is a further difficulty, which concerns the force of Malcolm's example. It is very difficult to imagine that someone might really offer a proof that 2 + 2 is not equal to 4. I can imagine that someone might *construct* such a proof with some strange premises. But I cannot imagine it should be meant to convince people that 2 + 2 does not equal 4 nor that anyone might be convinced by it. To imagine this one must suppose this arithmetical sentence having a use altogether different from the one it has. It must be imagined as something about which doubt and debate are acknowledged, and regarding which proof could be relevant. But if it were *such* a sen-

9. *Ibid.*, p. 63.

tence, it would not serve Malcolm as an illustration of what he knows in the strong sense! That is to say, on this assumption his attitude would presumably be different.

The sentence 'I know that $2 + 2 = 4$' is an exceedingly odd one to actually use. The oddness of it has to do with the fact that no one questions whether $2 + 2 = 4$, and that reflects in turn its perfect security. The difficulty here is related to the difficulty facing Moore when he wanted to give examples of what he knew; the security of our 'knowledge' of it counts against its being something we can say we know. To make it into something we might say is known is to make it into something it isn't. Such a simple arithmetical proposition does not serve to illustrate 'knowing' in any sense and so not in the strong one. Let us therefore look at a nonmathematical example Malcolm provides:

> Suppose that as I write this paper someone in the next room were to call out to me "I can't find an ink-bottle; is there one in the house?" I should reply "Here is an ink-bottle." If he said in a doubtful tone "Are you sure? I looked there before," I should reply "Yes, I know there is; come and get it."[10]

Does this example illustrate a natural and ordinary sense of 'know'?

Imagine the example changed in the following way: Imagine that Malcolm is *not* sitting at his desk but in his living room. When asked if he knows where there is an ink bottle, he replies that there is one on his desk. When asked again, he replies, "I *know* it's there—I just put it there!" This use of 'know' is entirely natural and it is emphatic, strong. But is it strong in Malcolm's sense? No. For in this situation Malcolm would not be willing to say that nothing could prove him mistaken or that no evidence would count against there being an ink bottle where he said one was. To introduce his 'strong' sense, Malcolm supposes that he is looking directly at or

10. *Ibid.*, p. 66.

touching what is unquestionably an ink bottle. But then his use of 'I know there is an ink-bottle here' is very odd.[11] We imagine him sitting and looking right at the object while he says it, and this is a curious performance—like a ceremony. The use becomes more natural as we imagine the ink bottle somewhere else, or we imagine the room is dark, or imagine some other condition raising the possibility that the speaker may be mistaken. But these conditions virtually exclude the use of 'know' in the strong sense! We are again faced with the dilemma that prevents there being examples of what we know: the highest grade of certainty belongs to propositions we don't use, or to propositions in circumstances where we don't use them. To use them where they are unshakably certain is unnatural. Malcolm tries to convince us that he knows there is an ink bottle in the strong sense of 'know' by asking: "Now could it turn out to be false that there is an ink-bottle directly in front of me on this desk?"[12] To which he answers, "No." But it is the wrong question, for it points to the utter security of Malcolm's 'knowledge,' and this defeats the claim that he might say he knows it. As Malcolm says, his strong sense of 'knows' *is* similar to the philosophical concept of perfect certainty. But like that concept it does not represent what is really meant by saying we know or by saying that something is certain.

2

When we say something is certain, we mean that our belief is secure. We would not use such a strong expression if

11. In another paper, "Defending Common Sense," (pp. 201–220), Malcolm argues that this sort of assertion *is* odd. He argues that there must be some occasion for doubt in order for 'I know' to be used correctly (esp. pp. 203ff.). His conditions for the correct use of 'know' are therefore stronger than mine; however, much of his argument agrees with mine of the following pages, and I confess that I have profited from puzzling over his mistakes.

12. *Knowledge and Certainty*, p. 68.

we did not mean that. Why should there be a problem in the concept of perfect certainty, a certainty that stands above the possibility of doubt? But perhaps there is a conflict here. If certainty belongs to the expression of belief, then is it not implied that whatever is called certain is really only a matter of belief? And if that is so, then does it not *follow* that no such matter stands beyond the possibility of doubt? That is to say, if something is a matter of belief, is it not *ipso facto* a matter that could be doubted?[13] If so, then there is a difficulty inherent in the concept of perfect certainty.

When we say a thing is certain we do so against some background. What kind? There is positively no point in asserting a thing against a background where no one could imaginably question it, dispute it, or wonder about it. When we say a thing is certain, therefore, we assume that not everyone believes and accepts it. This condition gives our remark its point and its function. But now have we not established an ultimate and indissoluble paradox, that a thing is called 'certain' only where it might be doubted, that what is certain—what is naturally so-called—is disputable? From this it plainly follows that there cannot be instances of perfectly certain knowledge if by this is meant knowledge everyone accepts and agrees to. The following example illustrates how this works.

Imagine that a defendant Suzie is being tried for stealing pearls. A witness is called to testify and testifies to the following: Suzie was seen wearing pearls at a party after the theft occurred but not before; Suzie could not have bought the pearls, since she never had more than $100 in her possession, while the pearls were known to be worth $1000; Suzie had been in the room where the pearls were kept at about the time of the theft. The witness is asked if this is all she knows, and replies that it is.

13. In "Defending Common Sense," Malcolm makes this point (pp. 203ff.).

Is there an argument for saying that she did not tell all she knew about the theft in testifying to these things? Could one argue: She did not say that Suzie is human, for example, although this seems to be implied; and she did not testify that 100 is less than 1000, although this too is implied by her testimony. If she did not know these things, her testimony is exceedingly shaky; if she did know them, why did she not testify to them?

Before we accept the excuse that the witness does not assert these things because they are 'obvious,' we should remember that many things testified to in court are obvious to anyone with common sense. The witness did not refrain from telling these things because they were unnecessary or boring, I propose, but for a much more important reason.

Imagine that on the contrary the witness *had* testified that Suzie is a human and not an automaton. This is written in the record. Is it a matter of indifference that it is there? The court assumed she was human, but there's no harm in giving proof for it, is there? Surprisingly there is. Consider the matter this way. What is written down as being testified to has a particular status. It is open to questioning, and evidence can be brought both for and against it. Imagine, then, that evidence is brought against the proposition that Suzie is human; then evidence is brought on the other side; the issue is debated. This becomes now one of the things the jury must decide about. If they decide negatively—that Suzie is not human but only an automaton—then one condition of criminal proceedings is missing and the case will be dismissed. But what brought this possible state of affairs into view? It was the assertion of the witness that Suzie is human and that she, the witness, knew as much.

The assertion that one knows a thing can have different functions on different occasions, as we have seen in earlier chapters. 'I know' contrasts with a variety of things: 'I don't know,' 'I only believe,' 'I haven't any idea,' 'I'm convinced of the opposite,' and so forth. It depends upon the circumstances what contrasts are being drawn. In its philosophical use, however such circumstances are lacking. How are we to understand the meaning of philosophical claims to know? We cannot suppose a philosopher asserts that he knows a thing in the way a student does in class, or in the way a chemist does after confirming an experimental finding, or in the way a mystic does. He asserts it without a background of debate. And he asserts it as being, in some sense, justified.

Consider this situation: A person mounts a soapbox and begins to assert a number of things. In the course of speaking he is interrupted with the question how he knows them. This challenge is appropriate. How can we say that? Because its appropriateness is established by the speaker's assertions. Now we often look at this pattern from the side of the questioner. We reason, if the speaker says such-and-such, have we not the right to question how he knows it? And the answer is: yes, we have such a right. It would be unreasonable for the speaker to say that such a challenge was out of order, inappropriate. For he has himself set the stage for it and sanctioned it. But when we are studying the nature of knowledge, we seem to be thinking of ourselves in the position of the speaker who wants to assert some things *without* acknowledging the legitimacy of a challenge. We want to assert things in a way that is *final*, with a tone of voice or manner or expression of speech that says: This issue is settled and may not be further considered. We want a certainty that is absolutely final. But what we want doesn't exist. There are (as we have seen) uses of 'know' which express impatience with debate and an unwillingness to argue further. But expressing these things does not close debate; it is better seen as part of it. So long as a thing is asserted or said to be known or to be certain, its denial and debate will necessarily be appropriate. This is a logical fact. For this is how 'I know' normally functions. It is how 'It's certain' functions too. And it is how 'It is absolutely certain, certain beyond any question and certain in the highest degree' functions as well. If one does not wish to have questions raised, one is advised not to use any such expressions as these. We cannot close debate with asseverations of certainty.

Instead of closing debate, our strong and emphatic claims to know a thing guarantee that the issue stays open. Therefore, the question with which we began—whether anything is absolutely certain, so certain that no reasonable man could doubt it—has a double significance. Viewed as a question whether we legitimately *say* in ordinary situations that something is certain, the answer is 'Yes.' There surely are times when this is quite appropriate, as when for instance a jury says that something is 'beyond any reasonable doubt.' But taken as a question whether anything is certain and being so actually stands above reasonable challenge and debate, the answer is 'No.' This is like asking if any silver is also gold, for what satisfies the one predicate will necessarily not satisfy the other.

This account of certainty explains a curious feature of those proofs of Moore's which contain assertions that some extremely obvious things are true and known by him. An instance of this is his holding up his hand and saying 'Here is a hand' and then saying this is something he knows. A natural response for a philosopher sitting in the audience is to ask how Moore knows this and whether he really does. But this response is at the same time ludicrous! What could Moore possibly do to answer such a question? Nothing. Therefore we might conclude that the questioner is playful, facetious, playing a philosophical game. Yet clearly this response *belongs* to this sort of situation. It belongs in settings where, against a background of debate, someone says a thing is so and he knows it is. What has gone wrong in this instance? The answer is that Moore's assertions were themselves wrong. They appeared to be eligible for debate and doubt but were not. Moore chose them because they were *not* susceptible to challenge. But then he offered them in a way which implied that they *were*. The initiation of doubt and questioning which attends that use was both unwanted and empty. No meaningful debate could ensue; but neither could Moore's assertions be treated as final.

Moore's assertions that he knew such obvious things could not be treated in the way assertions in ordinary discussions can. Yet we recognize the models on which they are formed, models that are insecure and disputable, subject to doubt and not at all capable of serving as good examples of what is known. We can best think of Moore's assertions as having a kind of ceremonial use. They lack the function of the original while calling our attention to it and reminding us of it, as Malcolm remarked.

3

The defense of knowledge against skepticism is a misguided venture. By claiming that some things are known and certainly known and unquestionable, we do not close the door against skepticism but keep it open. Then what can be said against the skeptic? Does it follow that skepticism is a coherent and reasonable position to hold? Can we do nothing to refute it?

Consider where skepticism enters. How and whether Moore knew the things he claimed to are questions arising after Moore asserted that he knew. Those questions *became* natural—acquired justification—in that way. They would not have been reasonable things to ask had he not made the assertions he did. Then should Moore not have asserted those things even though they refute the skeptical view? But they do not refute it; they legitimize it.

We must make clear what the skeptical position is; only then can we see whether it needs refuting and how that might be done. How shall we state that view? It is sometimes put like this: 'Doubt is always possible'; or 'Nothing is so certain it cannot be doubted'; or 'There is nothing we cannot doubt.'

These are extremely vague, however, and there is one thing at least which they should not mean, which if they do mean entails that they are false. They should not be taken to mean that, in every case where we express firm belief and claim to know or be certain of a thing, *we*—whoever is making the assertion—can doubt instead. Where we say that a thing is completely and utterly certain, we may and often do mean that *we* cannot conceive that it is not so. We may mean that we cannot ourselves imagine doubting it. This is something both Moore and Malcolm justly call attention to—that is, the fact that we cannot doubt everything that we think is certain. In the view of each of us some of the things we claim to know are incontrovertible, indubitable, utterly secure. I know of certain things that happened during my childhood, for example, and no adult testimony to the contrary, no evidence of any kind, can shake the security of these memories. If skepticism were the view that I *can* or might doubt such things as I hold with this certainty, then skepticism would be mistaken. And insofar as Descartes requires of himself and of us to doubt such things, he was insensitive to the fact that for each of us some things we claim to know are literally indubitable. The 'possibility' of doubting all that one has ever claimed to know is not a possibility at all.

Interpreting skepticism as saying that it is possible to doubt everything we know renders it false. But another interpretation of it is right: Whatever one asserts that he knows, or whatever he claims to be certain of, is a matter that someone may reasonably doubt. The reason for saying this is not acquaintance with human nature or a particular understanding of what it is to feel certainty or doubt. The reason is a logical one. The correct use of 'certain' is such that the reasonableness of doubt is assured by *saying* that a thing is certain. By 'reasonableness of doubt,' furthermore, one must understand that when I, for example, say a thing is certain, I acknowledge that a doubt may exist in someone's mind about it. I do not close my mind against this possibility or against someone having reasons to doubt. If my mind were so closed, then it would be inappropriate for me to say that I know it. It would be, like Malcolm's and Moore's examples, an incorrect case of 'knowing.'

Doubt about what someone claims to know is always reasonable from some point of view.[14] This does not count against our saying we know what we ordinarily claim to. On the contrary, it is a condition we acknowledge in saying we know, and necessary if our claims to know are to have their full force. That doubt is always possible regarding what we know, or claim to know, is a logical truth; it says something about the connection between the concepts 'knowledge' and 'possible doubt.' Specifically it says they are inseparable.

There is no defense against the possibility of doubt. We can see now why it is so easy to raise skeptical questions against something proffered as knowledge. For the usual response is: But might someone not have evidence against it, and so not accept this as knowledge, as you claim it is? Of course, someone might! That is not surprising, but only one mark of a good instance in which something is said to be known. It follows that skepticism, correctly understood, is irrefutable, but also that it is harmless.

Our concern about skepticism and the demand for absolute certainty arise because we misread how our language works. If someone says, 'This is absolutely certain—certain beyond doubt or the possibility of doubt,' he is expressing his belief. He does not describe a state of affairs when he says it is certain; nor does he assume others must agree with him that it is certain. Yet that's how it sounds. So we are surprised when we realize how easy it is to inject a doubt against any purported 'certainty.' This seems to show that the certainty was

14. I am speaking here and hereafter of knowing as it belongs in a context of debate and discussion, leaving aside the uses that are irrelevant to the issue of skepticism.

not absolute, and by generalization that no certainty is. But doubt belongs to the language of belief-expression no less than certainty does. Doubt-expression belongs to the same part of language. Skepticism and certainty are aspects of the same picture.

4

I turn to relate the above conclusions to the attempt to define knowledge in terms of necessary and sufficient conditions. Such a definition is given by Chisholm:

"S knows that *h* is true" means (i) S accepts *h*; (ii) S has adequate evidence for *h*; and (iii) *h* is true.[15]

The purpose of this definition is to assure us that there can and should be agreement about what is known. Giving necessary and sufficient conditions for whether someone knows a thing is treating this concept like the concept 'zebra.' It is to encourage the idea that an instance either falls under the concept of 'knowing' or it does not. And in so doing, it encourages us to think that the concept is objective and that a concensus about what is known is not less plausible than a concensus about what animals are zebras.

This attempt to define knowledge embodies the same mistake as does the search for absolute certainty. It supposes that we need to determine what is known unequivocally, if knowing is the important and useful concept we think it to be. However, claiming to know a thing is not like identifying something. We do not have necessary and sufficient conditions for knowing because, instead of identifying a kind of thing, we are thereby expressing our beliefs, giving assurance, supplying information, and so on. Our assertions about knowing serve a variety of functions. We don't always or even generally expect others to agree about what we say we know. We don't generally expect people to take our word for what

15. *Op. cit.*, p. 16.

we say we know; some will trust our judgment, but others will not. Last, that we speak and understand the same language does not foster agreement about what is known, as it does about what is called a 'zebra.' These features show what we have seen to be true already: that saying one knows a thing is not subsuming it under a class concept.

That 'know' serves as an expression of belief accounts for several difficulties in the definitional approach to knowledge. For whether someone *does have* 'adequate evidence,' whether he *does* 'accept *h*,' and whether *h is true*—all these reflect *our beliefs*. These cannot be determined 'objectively' if that means determining them without regard for our beliefs. That is logically impossible! At the same time there is no reason why we must look for a concensus. On the contrary, whatever is naturally claimed to be known may not *ipso facto* be a subject of universal agreement. 'Knowledge' belongs to the sphere of debate, challenge, inquiry, proof; that is its logical home. It does not belong where there is final and unquestioned authority; it belongs where there are differences and controversy.[16]

The philosophy of knowledge should not be concerned with what is certain and how we know it is. The question: What do we know and is it certain? sounds like: What kinds of sea mammals are there and how do we find them? But the similarity is deceptive. There is no collection of things known, and there are no means for 'identifying' what is known. Whatever fact I offer as an interesting example of what I know will surely admit of contravention; this circumstance does not reflect on my example but rather on the concept of knowing. And it would be foolish if we were to replace this

16. There is probably a connection between this argument and the arguments for saying some concepts are "essentially contestable," a connection suggested to me by Elizabeth Beardsley. I refer the reader to A. McIntyre, "The Essential Contestability of Some Social Concepts," *Ethics*, 84 (Oct. 1973), pp. 1–9, for clarification and further references.

example with a surer fact, for then we mislead ourselves about what we are studying. The question 'What do we know?' gives us an utterly wrong picture of knowledge. No wonder we are confused trying to answer it!

The right subject of the philosophy of knowledge is 'know' as it functions in ordinary settings and everyday affairs. When we leave these functions behind and turn to what is surer and more indubitable, we also leave the meaning of 'know' behind. We may of course find some propositions with unusual properties, for example, that one exists, that time is real. But these are curiosities. They have no profound implications for knowledge, and they do not reveal anything about the 'structure' of knowledge or beliefs. What relates to knowledge stands in a more precarious place, neither so secure nor so uninteresting, and never beyond the general possibility of doubt.

Bibliography of Works Cited

Books

Aristotle. *Metaphysics*. R. Hope, trans. Ann Arbor, 1968.
——. *Physics*. R. McKeon, ed. New York, 1941.
Austin, John. *Philosophical Papers*. London, 1961.
Bradley, F. H. *Appearance and Reality*. Oxford, 1951.
——. *Presuppositions of Critical History*. Chicago, 1968.
Broad, C. D. *Mind and Its Place in Nature*. New York, 1951.
Chisholm, Roderick. *Perceiving*. Ithaca, N.Y., 1957.
Descartes, René. *Descartes: Philosophical Writings*. G. E. M. Anscombe and P. Geach, trans. and eds. Edinburgh, 1954.
——. *The Philosophical Works of Descartes*. E. Haldane and G. R. T. Ross, trans. Cambridge, 1967.
Doney, Willis, ed. *Descartes*. Garden City, N.Y., 1967.
Frankfurt, Harry. *Demons, Dreamers and Madmen*. New York, 1967.
Galilei, G. *The Two New Sciences*. H. Drew and A. de Salvio, trans. New York, 1914.
Griffiths, A. P., ed. *Knowledge and Belief*. London, 1967.
Harman, G. and D. Davidson, eds. *Semantics of Natural Language*. Dordrecht, 1972.
Hintikka, Jaakko. *Knowledge and Belief*. Ithaca, N.Y., 1962.
Hume, David. *Enquiries Concerning the Human Understanding*. L. A. Selby-Bigge, ed. 2d ed., London, 1951.
Kant, Immanuel. *Critique of Pure Reason*. N. K. Smith, trans. New York, 1965.
Kenny, Anthony. *Descartes*. New York, 1968.

Lewis, C. I. *Mind and the World Order*. New York, 1956.

Locke John. *Essay Concerning Human Understanding*. New York, 1964.

Malcolm, Norman. *Knowledge and Certainty*. Englewood Cliffs, N.J., 1963.

McTaggart, James. *Philosophical Studies*. New York, 1966.

Moore, G. E. *Commonplace Book: 1919–1953*. London, 1962.

——. *Ethics*. London, 1949.

——. *Lectures on Philosophy*. C. Lewy, ed. London, 1966.

——. *Philosophical Papers*. London, 1959.

——. *Philosophical Studies*. London, 1948.

——. *Some Main Problems of Philosophy*. London, 1953.

Plato. *The Dialogues of Plato*. B. Jowett, trans. New York, 1937.

Price, H. H. *Belief*. London, 1969.

Prichard, H. A. *Knowledge and Perception*. London, 1950.

Rhees, Rush. *Discussions of Wittgenstein*. London, 1970.

Russell, Bertrand. *The Problems of Philosophy*. London, 1959.

Schilpp, Paul, ed. *The Philosophy of G. E. Moore*. New York, 1952.

Searle, John. *Speech Acts*. Cambridge, 1970.

Stevenson, C. L. *Ethics and Language*. New Haven, 1944.

Strawson, P. F. *Introduction to Logical Theory*. London, 1952.

——. *Logico Linguistic Papers*. London, 1971.

Wittgenstein, Ludwig. *The Blue and Brown Books*. New York, 1958.

——. *Lectures and Conversations on Aesthetics, Psychology and Religious Belief*. C. Barrett, ed. Berkeley, 1967.

——. *On Certainty*. G. E. M. Anscombe and G. H. von Wright, eds. New York, 1969.

——. *Philosophical Investigations*. G. E. M. Anscombe, trans. Oxford, 1953.

——. *Remarks on the Foundations of Mathematics*. Oxford, 1956.

Articles

Ambrose, Alice. "Commanding a Clear View of Philosophy," Presidential Address, American Philosophical Association Meetings, New York, 1975.

Black, Max. "On Speaking with the Vulgar," *Philosophical Review* 58 (Nov. 1949).

——. "Saying and Disbelieving," Analysis, 13 (Dec. 1952).

Campbell, C. A. "Common Sense Propositions and Philosophical Paradoxes," *Proceedings of the Aristotelian Society*, 45 (1944/45).

Coder, David. "Thalberg's Defense of Justified True Belief," *Journal of Philosophy*, 67 (June 1970).

Hintikka, Jaakko. "Cogito, Ergo Sum: Inference or Performance?" in W. Doney, ed., *Descartes*.

Klein, Peter. "A Proposed Definition of Propositional Knowledge," *Journal of Philosophy*, 68 (Aug. 1971).

Kripke, Saul. "Naming and Necessity," in G. Harman and D. Davidson, eds., *Semantics of Natural Language*.

Malcolm, Norman. "Descartes' Proof that His Essence is Thinking," in W. Doney, ed., *Descartes*.

——. "Defending Common Sense," *Philosophic Review*, 58 (May 1949).

——. "George Edward Moore," in *Knowledge and Certainty*.

——. "Knowledge and Belief," in *Knowledge and Certainty*.

——. "Moore and Ordinary Language," in P. Schilpp, ed., *The Philosophy of G. E. Moore*.

McIntyre, Alisdair. "The Contestability of Some Social Concepts," *Ethics*, 84 (Oct. 1973).

Moore, G. E. "A Reply to My Critics," in P. Schilpp, ed., *The Philosophy of G. E. Moore*.

Price, H. H. "Some Considerations about Belief," in A. P. Griffiths, ed., *Knowledge and Belief*.

Radford, Colin. "Knowledge by Examples," *Analysis*, 27 (Oct. 1966).

van Fraassen, Bas. "Presupposition, Implication, and Self-Reference," *Journal of Philosophy*, 65 (Mar. 1968).

White, Alan. "Certainty," *Aristotelian Society Supplementary Volume*, 46 (1972).

——. "What We Believe," in *Studies in the Philosophy of Mind*, American Philosophical Quarterly Monograph No. 6 (Oxford, 1972).

Wolgast, Elizabeth. "Knowing and What It Implies," *Philosophical Review* 81 (July 1971), 360–370.

Index of Names

Index

Paradoxes of Knowledge

Designed by R. E. Rosenbaum.
Composed by York Composition Company, Inc.,
in 11 point Linotype Janson, 2 points leaded,
with display lines in monotype Deepdene.
Printed letterpress from type by York Composition Company
on Warren's Number 66 text, 50 pound basis.
Bound by John H. Dekker & Sons, Inc.
in Joanna book cloth
and stamped in All Purpose foil.

Library of Congress Cataloging in Publication Data
(For library cataloging purposes only)

Wolgast, Elizabeth Hankins, 1929–
    Paradoxes of knowledge.

    Bibliography: p.
    Includes index.
    1. Belief and doubt. 2. Paradox. 3. Knowledge, Theory of.
I. Title.
BD215.W63   121   77-3130
ISBN 0-8014-1090-8